Devdutt Pattanaik

The Man Who Was a Woman and Other Queer Tales from Hindu Lore

*Pre-publication
REVIEWS,
COMMENTARIES,
EVALUATIONS . . .*

"The Man Who Was a Woman retells all of my favorite stories of sexual ambiguity in a readable, easily accessible way. No heavy doses of theory get in the way of the stories, but the lightest dusting of queer theory brings the book into line with other, more ponderous works. It will be an ideal text for courses on gender and queer studies, and students will love it."

Wendy Doniger O'Flaherty
Author, *Hindu Myths:
A Sourcebook, Translated from
the Sanskrit; The Rig Veda: An Anthology;*
and *Women, Androgynes, and Other
Mythical Beasts*

"Devdutt Pattanaik has done important research to gather multiple references to gender and sexual variance in Hindu traditions. Only a writer who is intimately familiar with the many thousands of Hindu legends could compile this book. Pattanaik not only quotes the legends themselves, but also offers his own extensive commentary to place the stories in proper context.

Though Hinduism strongly promotes heterosexual procreation, it also offers many 'queer' examples of transgenderism and same-sex love that break free of the binary heterosexual mold. It is important for India to reclaim these precolonial traditions and adapt them for the realities facing an overpopulated nation in the twenty-first century. Since Hindu lore recognizes that social law must change with time to meet the demands of a particular age, nonprocreative sex has the potential to become accepted as a natural element of the manifestation of the divine. Hindu ideas of divine androgyny offer a basis for greater acceptance of gender diversity in the future."

Walter L. Williams, PhD
Professor of Anthropology
and Gender Studies,
University of Southern California;
Editor, *International Gay
and Lesbian Review*

The Man Who Was a Woman and Other Queer Tales from Hindu Lore

HAWORTH GAY & LESBIAN STUDIES
John P. De Cecco, PhD
Editor in Chief

The Man Who Was a Woman and Other Queer Tales from Hindu Lore

Devdutt Pattanaik

Harrington Park Press®
An Imprint of The Haworth Press, Inc.
New York • London • Oxford

The man who was a
woman and other
queer tales of Hindu
lore

Published by

Harrington Park Press®, an imprint of The Haworth Press, Inc., 10 Alice Street, Binghamton, NY
13904-1580

Cover design by Marylouise E. Doyle.

The cover is a twentieth-century calendar reprint of a medieval Pahari painting (c. 1800 C.E.) show-
ing Krishna, the most perfect earthly incarnation of the divine, letting his female companions adorn
him as a woman. This was part of Krishna's leela, divine game, played during his stay in Gokula, the
village of cowherds and milkmaids. On one hand it can be seen as an endearing submission of the
beloved to the whims of his lovers during the festival of colors, Holi, when convention is abandoned
and the eroticism of nature celebrated with the coming of spring. On another, it can be interpreted as
an enactment of a thought Krishna expresses later in life in the *Bhagavad Gita:* "The body is nothing
but a garment of the soul, worn afresh at birth and discarded at death." Woman or man, in apparel, biology, or behavior, the divine within remains unaffected and unruffled, awaiting discovery by all.

Library of Congress Cataloging-in-Publication Data

The man who was a woman and other queer tales of Hindu lore / [compiled by] Devdutt Pattanaik.
    p. cm.
    Includes bibliographical references and index.
    ISBN 1-56023-180-7 (hard : alk. paper)—ISBN 1-56023-181-5 (soft : alk. paper)
    1. Sex role—Religious aspects—Hinduism. 2. Hinduism—Doctrines. 3. Transvestism—Religious
aspects—Hinduism. 4. Hindu literature—History and criticism. I. Pattanaik, Devdutt.

BL1215.S49 M36 2001
294.5'13—dc21

2001016663

For
everyone who believes
in possibilities and choices

ABOUT THE AUTHOR

Dr. Devdutt Pattanaik, MBBS, graduated in medicine from Grant Medical College, Mumbai, and went on to specialize in the field of medical writing and health communication. With a passion for mythology, he topped the Mumbai University course in comparative mythology (PGDCM) and has published four books on the subject: *Shiva: An Introduction; Vishnu: An Introduction; Devi: An Introduction;* and *Goddess in India: Five Faces of the Eternal Feminine. Hanuman: An Introduction* and *Mysteries of Hindu Mythology* are forthcoming.

Dr. Pattanaik is part of 'Sabrang,' a cultural organization that demystifies the arts, and has lectured extensively on the relevance of mythology to modern man. His articles have been published in the *Times of India* "Speaking Tree." His essay "Threshold of Chastity" can be found in the Spring 2000 issue of Parabola [www.parabola.org].

Dr. Pattanaik lives in India.

CONTENTS

Preface

Every culture has sacred narratives that capture its worldview. Among them, one occasionally finds stories that seem to rupture the traditional discourse. This book compiles such "subversive" stories related to sex and gender from Hindu lore.

An attempt is made to explain the presence of such "queer" narratives within the grand religious canvas, keeping in mind the complex and ambiguous relationship between pleasure, fertility, and celibacy in the Hindu construct, the ritual and symbolic role of men and women, the existence of nonconventional gender constructs in traditional society, the generally disdainful response to them by the Hindu bourgeoisie, and the increasingly expressive queer and L/G/B/T movements in modern India.

Further, this book aims to demonstrate that there is no timeless and universal attitude toward things queer. Different cultures express and repress sexuality in different ways in different times. In doing so, the book makes a case against the quest for "a normal and natural Utopia" where there is one reality, one logic, one law, one worldview, and one way of life.

Devdutt Pattanaik

Acknowledgments

I would like to thank the following for their help in making this book a reality:

- My parents, for supporting this book and enduring my creative pangs
- Nimu, for enriching and empowering my life
- Ashok, who clarified why *maya* means "delusion," not "illusion," thus sparking off a series of ideas
- Barbara Lloyd, for giving me permission to use the photo of the Jogappa from her book *Colours of Southern India,* published by Thames and Hudson
- Dolf Hartsuiker, for giving me permission to use the photo of the Sakhi from his book *Sadhus,* published by Thames and Hudson
- Aniruddha, for letting me use the photograph he clicked at Khajuraho, Madhya Pradesh
- Rajiv and Sachin, for digging out relevant information from the Internet
- Quentin, for his valuable insights after reading the preface
- Ramki, for throwing light on terminologies related to queer studies
- Nikita, for introducing me to postmodern vocabulary
- Lakshmi, for giving me access to lesser-known Tamil temple lore
- The scholars who have painstakingly compiled, translated, and analyzed Hindu lore that would otherwise have remained unheard
- That nameless person who once asked the question, "What makes me human, being a man or being a woman?"

Introduction:
Placing Stories in Context

A god transforms into a nymph and enchants another god. A king becomes pregnant. Another king has children who call him "father," and "mother." A hero turns into a eunuch and wears female apparel. A prince discovers on his wedding night that he is not a man. A princess has to turn into a man before she can avenge her humiliation. Widows of a king make love to conceive his child. Friends of the same sex end up marrying each other after one of them metamorphoses into a woman. These are some of the tales I came upon in my study of Hindu lore. They may be viewed as queer. Queer, because they break free from the binary heterosexual mold that dominates Hindu society.

In this book, I have compiled tales from Hindu lore that revolve around the theme of sexual transformation and gender metamorphosis. By sex, I mean biology. By gender, I mean social expression of that biology through apparel and mannerisms. Anatomy, apparel, and behavior are easier to identify in a narrative, leaving the underlying psychology open to all forms of interpretation. One can only speculate on the sexual orientation and gender identity of the characters, because in all these stories the narrative rarely dwells on desires and fantasies of the protagonist. Also, sexual attraction between characters is generally expressed in heterosexual terms: a man is never attracted to a man, until one of them "becomes a woman."

UNIVERSALITY OF QUEER NARRATIVES

The themes of sexual transformation and gender metamorphosis are not unique to Hindu lore. In Greek lore, for example, one comes upon the tale of the seer Teiresias who lived his life both as a man and as a woman. The story goes that once, on coming upon a pair of copulating serpents, Teiresias killed the female of the pair and was cursed by her mate to turn into a woman. Seven years later, on coming upon another pair of copulating serpents, Teiresias killed the male and regained his manhood. Having had sex both as a man and as a woman made him the perfect arbiter in a dispute between Zeus, the king of the gods, and his queen Hera, as to whether man or woman gained more pleasure from sexual intercourse. Teiresias answered, "Woman," angering Hera, who struck him blind, and pleasing Zeus, who gave him long life and the gift of prophecy. Zeus, himself, turned into a woman—the very likeness of Artemis, the goddess of the chase, renowned for her homoerotic affections—to get close to and seduce the nymph Callisto. The Greeks also knew the cross-dressing hero. The mighty Hercules spent a year dressed as a woman in the court of Queen Omphale. The Nereid Thetis dressed her son Achilles in woman's clothes and hid him in the female quarters, lest the Achaeans recruit him in the ill-fated Trojan campaign.[1]

There is an Irish folklore of the handsome young abbot of Drimnagh who turned into a woman while resting on a mound. As a woman, he could not return to his wife. So he left his village, went to another village where he fell in love with a handsome young man, got married, had seven children, and lived the life of a housewife for seven years. In his eighth year as a woman, his family was invited to Drimnagh for the Easter feast. On the way, he took a nap. When he awoke, he had turned into a man once again. On one side stood his wife, on the other stood his husband and their seven children. What was he to do? The court came to his aid and gave him custody of three of his children. The abbot returned to his wife, but remained friends with his "husband" for the rest of his life. Though the protagonist of this tale is an abbot, the tale has nothing to do with Christianity. The tale's pre-Christian origin is suggested when the people of the area accept the event as a trick of the mysterious "little people" or fairies who populate the Irish countryside.[2]

DIFFERENCES IN QUEER NARRATIVES

I believe that homoeroticism, simply defined as sexual chemistry between members of the same sex, is a universal phenomenon. Society, however, with its foundations in patriarchy and heterosexuality, controls its expression so that it does not threaten the dominant discourse. In different societies, homoerotic tendencies express themselves in different ways, ways that may be viewed as "queer." These queer manifestations of sexuality, though repressed socially, squeeze their way into the myths, legends, and lore of the land.

Myths, legend, and lore capture the collective unconscious of a people. They are revered inheritances, a complex weave of ancient attitudes and ambitions. Deemed sacred, they generate a worldview for a people, explain the inexplicable, and give life meaning, direction, and certainty. To understand the unexpressed worlds of a people, to decipher coping skills of a culture, an unraveling of myth, a decoding of lore is essential.

Greek tales of sexual transformation and gender metamorphosis are neither as common nor as popular as Greek tales of man-boy love. Almost every Greek god and Greek hero had an erotic relationship with a boy.[3] Zeus was so infatuated with Ganymede, prince of Troy, that he took the form of an eagle, abducted the boy from his cradle, appointed him cupbearer in Olympus, and finally cast him in the starry sky as the constellation Aquarius. Poseidon—lord of the seas—found his own cupbearer and bedfellow in Pelops, prince of Lydia. The sun-god Apollo fought the poet Thamyris and the wind-god Zephyrus for the love of the beautiful lad, Hyacinthus. Hercules abandoned the Argonaut mission distraught at the disappearance of his beloved Hylas. Greek gods and heroes did not have to "become women" in order to lay with boys. The Greeks apparently despised the very idea of cross-dressing and effeminacy. The love of a man for a boy, however, was institutionalized. This socially approved pedophilic expression of homoeroticism reflected itself in the lore of the land.[4]

In Hindu narratives, gods and heroes never abduct young boys in a romantic frenzy. They do "become women," however, either biologically (sex change) or cosmetically (cross-dressing), to tempt hermits or to trick demons. What does this tell us about Hindu attitudes toward queer sexuality?

One will not find tales of sexual transformation and gender metamorphosis in the Bible. It will be considered blasphemous even to think of a patriarch in women's clothes or to adore a prophet for having lived his life both as a man and as a woman. Hindus, on the other hand, venerate Shiva, who is Ardhanareshwara, the half-woman god.

HINDU VERSUS BIBLICAL PARADIGM

When I read the Bible for the first time, I was struck by the linearity of narrative, consistency of plot, and compartmentalization of gender. As the narrative unfolded itself, I was swept into a world where there is only one god, only one lifetime, and only one way of living one's life—by obeying the will of God. Existence is projected as profane, resulting from the sin of transgression. Life is nothing but the quest to return to primal purity by obeying the commandments of a male god revealed through a male prophet and by accepting his male offspring as the savior.

This was in stark contrast to what I experienced when I read Hindu lore. In the Hindu worldview, the world one lives in is just one of the innumerable worlds that exist in time and space. One's view of things is just one of the innumerable views floating around in the cosmos. Nothing in this manifold universe is absolute, except the unfathomable divine principle (addressed in early Hindu texts such as *Upanishads* as *brahman*). Everything is a manifestation of that divine principle. In the *Puranas,* Agamas, and Tantras, which are later Hindu texts, the divine principle is visualized as male *(Vishnu),* female *(Shakti),* or both *(Shiva).* The impression created is that life is a journey that does not begin with birth or end with death. There is no one "big bang" or one "apocalypse." Instead, there are innumerable days of doom and countless days of creation, alternating with unfailing regularity in the ever-turning, ever-transforming cosmic merry-go-round. As one oscillates between the land of the dead and the land of the living, genders change, orientations change, identities change—the future being determined by the past. Masculinity and femininity are reduced to ephemeral robes of body and mind that ensheath the sexless, genderless soul. The ultimate aim in the journey of life then becomes an exercise in appreciating the beauty of existence, understanding its limitations, before finally transcending it.

The difference between Hindu and biblical worldviews is manifest in their respective lore. Unlike most biblical narratives, every Hindu tale has several versions, innumerable interpretations, and no specific place in the religious canon. In these tales, legend and allegory move side by side. Symbols and metaphors mingle and merge with characters and plots. Idea and imagination thrive on the roller coaster of transmigration and the fluidity of identities. Locked within the tales of gods, kings, and sages are the blazing philosophies of ancient spiritual masters—the *yogis, siddhas, nathas,* and *acharyas.* Adapted by mystics, narrated by poets, expressed in both classical and vernacular dialects, the tales have, over the centuries, become integral parts of the Hindu spiritual landscape. The narratives are not simple parables or entertaining fables. Woven in the fantastic plots are concepts that form the core of the Hindu worldview—*karma* (determinism through past action), *dharma* (laws of cosmic and social stability), *maya* (delusion due to limited perception of the unenlightened mind), *samsara* (wheel of rebirths, cycle of material existence where everything is impermanent and recurrent), *moksha* (liberation from delusion and, hence, material existence). As one internalizes the tales, one comes to accept a universe that is boundlessly various, where everything occurs simultaneously, where all possibilities exist without excluding one another.

It is not surprising to find in Hindu scriptures tales of masculine goddesses and feminine gods, of men who become women and women who become men, of kings who become pregnant and heroes who cross-dress. The entire sexual spectrum and gender fluidity seems to have been captured. Whether this was the intention of the primal bard, we will never know. What we do know is that many gays, lesbians, bisexuals, and transgender people of Indian origin have found, and many more continue to find, resonance of their sexuality in these tales and derive strength from it.

STRUCTURED SOCIETY WITHIN FLUID PHILOSOPHY

Most Hindus are familiar with, and quite often enjoy, tales with sexually ambiguous themes. The masculinity of a hero is never threatened when he dons female attire. No one censors the tale of a man who becomes a woman. No one is offended by the tale of the woman who marries another woman. Indeed, a god's androgyny makes him worthy of adoration.

This, however, does not mean that the average Hindu is comfortable with "queer" identities. It must be kept in mind that despite the plurality in the philosophy, most Hindus follow a *parampara* or belong to a *sampradaya* with rules and codes of conduct fixed either by caste or by the guru. There are several traditions and religious orders in India, each one offering the follower a sense of certainty that would otherwise be overwhelmed by the celebration of universal flux found in scriptures. Hence the difference between scriptural concepts and social practice, between the classical or *margi* discourse on the fluidity of the cosmos and folk or *desi* belief in the rigidity of society.

While most Hindu philosophers acknowledge the existence of the female principle in men and the male principle in women, Hindu society does not take kindly to public display of the "alternative" self. When a male ascetic of the esoteric *Sakhi-bhava* order dresses up as a woman in order to be closer to the supreme divine principle who is perceived as the male god Krishna, he often ends becoming the object of amusement and ridicule rather than awe and appreciation. The average Vaishnava family, while fervently worshipping Krishna, whose gender-bending exploits are renowned (and retold in this book), would not empathize with their son's desire to become a Sakhi.

Most Hindus take tales of sexual transformation at face value or treat it with indifference. No one tries to find anything of deeper "sexual" significance in them. Few see them as tools to explore what one New Age scholar described as the "omnierotic and pangendered" nature of life and divinity.[5] They are certainly not seen as outpourings of the "queer" psyche. Any attempt to interpret them thus is met with hostility, branded as "perverted interpretations born of Western minds," and dismissed with disdain. When the nonheterosexual aspects of the narrative are pointed out, the general tendency is to exile the plots into the realm of sacrality ("that's the way of god, not man"), philosophy ("the tale should be seen allegorically, not literally"), metaphysics ("that's divine delusion, not divine direction"), comedy ("that's supposed to be funny, not real"), or fantasy ("it's just entertainment, don't take it so seriously").

THE HINDU WAY OF LIFE

The divide between Hindu philosophy and Hindu tradition is fascinating. It was even pointed out by Islamic scholar Al Beruni who visited India a thousand years ago.[6] While the philosophy acknowledges the essential equality of all human beings as containers of the divine spark, the society establishes itself through a rigid caste hierarchy, with caste—that is determined by birth—defining one's social status. While the philosophy accepts the boundless possibilities within the universe, the society binds every man and woman with duties as it transforms itself into a rigid heterosexual and patriarchal construct.

For the sake of social stability, scriptures demand unquestioning obedience to sacred duties (dharma) that are determined by one's inherited caste *(varna)* and one's stage in life *(ashrama)*. One duty, or rather a biological obligation, common to all castes, is to produce children so as to facilitate the rebirth of ancestors and keep the cycle of life rotating. It is considered a debt to one's forefathers that is incurred at birth. In the *Bhagavad Gita,* Krishna in his role as the preserver of cosmic and social order, expounds the virtue of dharma and identifies himself with procreative intercourse. He says in Chapter 7, verse 11: "I am sex life which is not contrary to religious principles (dharma)."[7] Another translation of the line by Professors Vrinda Nabar and Shanta Tumkur [Wordsworth Classics] reads: "I am also that desire in all created beings that is not inimical to immorality."[8]

So important is the need to father children that in ancient law books known as *Dharmashastras*, any man who could not participate in heterosexual intercourse (because of castration, impotency, or homosexuality) was referred to as a *kliba* and condemned by all. In the *Manusmriti* (c. 500 C.E.), the most renowned law book, the kliba is excluded from inheritance, sacrifice, and rituals. Chapter 3, verse 150, of the scripture reads: "Priests who steal, fallen men, non-men (impotent men), atheists (those who do not consider Vedas to be divine revelations) are unworthy of making offerings to the gods and ancestors."[9] In the epic *Mahabharata,* written nearly 2,000 years ago, men who cannot have sex with their wives or are unable to produce children for whatever reason are advised to nominate someone else, either a brother or a sage, to do the needful.

Though seemingly obsessed with dharma, the Hindu way of life also acknowledges the human need to earn a living *(artha)* and enjoy life *(kama)*. However, the right to worldly goods and worldly pleasures comes only *after* worldly duties are performed. Thus, marriage is transformed into the key to worldly life. Unless married, the Hindu man has no right to own property or perform religious rituals. He has no right to indulge his senses. The unmarried man is given only two choices: remain a chaste student *(brahmachari)* or turn into a celibate hermit *(sanyasi)*.

The burning issue among Hindu gays and lesbians is, not surprisingly, marriage. All hell breaks loose in a Hindu household not so much when a son or daughter displays homosexual tendencies, but when those tendencies come in the way of heterosexual marriage.

Similar to the sexually ambiguous tales narrated in the book, non-heterosexuality is ignored or tolerated so long as it does not upset the heterosexual world order.

The *Kamasutra* (c. 400 C.E.), a manual of erotica, apparently of divine origin, is one of the earliest Hindu manuals to prescribe non-procreative sexual activities, such as kissing and oral sex, for recreational purposes. Kama refers to a whole range of pleasures—visual, auditory, gustatory, aromatic, tactile, and, of course, erotic. Unlike dharma, which is concerned only with procreation, kama sex is linked to passion and pleasure. A celibate monk did not risk his chastity if he indulged only in dharma sex. Passionate and pleasurable sex was reserved for the gods and the worldly man. But passionate and pleasurable sex with whom? Men or women?

Logically, nonprocreative heterosexual sexual activity can be lumped in the same category as homosexual sexual activity. Both are forms of kama, nothing more. Both are sterile and both satisfy lust. This may be the reason why same-sex activity, when referred to, is never condemned with threats of "fire and brimstone" by Hindu seers. The concept of "eternal damnation" does not exist in Hinduism, as it does in Christianity. The Hindu world is not based on commandments and transgressions; it is based on karma, the law of action. The future depends on actions performed in the present. Failure to produce children can land a man in the realm known as *Put*, a place of great suffering, in one's next life with no hope of rebirth. If karma is judged to be good or bad depending on results, then—considering the result—failure to produce children is bad karma. But there is no scripture that specifically refers to same-sex activity as generating bad karma. As with all actions, it fetters one in the wheel of existence. Liberation or moksha—the ultimate goal of every living creature—comes only when one breaks free from the compulsion of wanting to react to worldly circumstances. Liberation comes from freedom from action, when one transcends desire, for man, and for woman.

HINDU RESPONSE TO QUEER SEXUALITY

For society, bad karma is that which threatens social stability. In a heterosexual and patriarchal construct, sex change, cross-dressing, same-sex intercourse, and other "queer" activities are bound to be considered undesirable, as they threaten the dominant discourse. Unlike marriage that brings about an acceptable compromise between the twin goals of procreation (for dharma) and renunciation (for moksha), homosexual union brings together two ritually polluting factors: sterility and lust.

In the *Manusmriti,* which lays down rules of conduct from an orthodox Brahmanical perspective, same-sex activity between men is condemned in the same breath that condemns injury to a priest, "smelling wine and things that are not to be smelled,"[10] incest, bestiality, anal and oral sex with a woman, vaginal sex with a menstruating woman, sex during the day. Punishments include "bathing with clothes on"; fasting; purifying oneself by consuming five cow products (cow's urine, dung, milk, curd, and butter); and social ostracization through "loss of caste." In the *Puranas* (c. 500 to 1500 C.E.), it is said that the breaking of caste rules as well as discharging semen in anything but the vagina lands a man in one of the many nether regions of the Hindu universe, where he has to suffer for seven years before he is reborn as a lesser being on earth when the cosmos are recreated. The *Narada Purana* (15:93-95) states: "The great sinner who discharges semen in non-vaginas, in those who are destitute of vulva, and wombs of animals shall fall into the nether realms where he shall subsist on semen and where he will remain for seven divine years before being reborn as a lowly man."[11]

Despite these scriptural injunctions against most things queer, it must be noted that Hindu scriptures do not serve the same purpose as the Bible in Christianity or the Koran in Islam. Most Hindu scriptures are *smriti,* arising from human memory, not divine will, hence open to rejection and modification. Only the Vedic texts are *shruti,* divine revelations. The *Vedas* (or books of cosmic wisdom) are concerned not with mundane human values, but with eternal and absolute truth. They are concerned with the nature of reality, the value of fertility, and the cycle of life, not with passion or pleasure, be it heterosexual, bisexual, or homosexual. What the *Upanishads* (philosophical treatises based on the *Vedas*) do say is that *everything* in this world is part of divinity and part of the age one lives in. Thus, the biblical concept of "evil" (everything that is devoid of godliness) makes no sense in the Hindu worldview.

Same-sex intercourse in modern India, though widely prevalent, is rarely "seen." If seen, it is rarely perceived as "sex." Many prefer to refer to it as *masti* (Hindi for fun, mischief) or *shauk* (Urdu for hobby, pleasurable pastime). Intercourse is viewed as a form of kama, nothing more. Privately, many men may indulge in it. Publicly, it may be seen as a "bad habit," similar to consuming alcohol, chewing tobacco, and visiting prostitutes—best avoided or ignored. Rarely is it qualified on "moral" terms. Intercourse is never termed *paap*, or an act that generates bad karma. It is seen as an act that brings dishonor, not damnation, to the family. Hence, in a homophobic environment, while homoerotically inclined Christians experience guilt, homoerotically inclined Hindus experience shame.

ADOPTION OF THE COLONIAL DISCOURSE

Pan-Indian laws that look upon nonvaginal intercourse as "unnatural" and cross-dressing as "offensive and obscene," came from the colonial masters of the land. In the nineteenth century, the British passed sodomy laws condemning anal and oral sex in biblical terms. When India attained independence, these laws were accepted without pause or consideration by those who framed the Indian constitution. As a result, traditional gender constructs and sexual behaviors, condemned by the colonial discourse, became illegal in the republic. A blind eye was turned toward depictions of "unnatural" sex on temple walls and of transgender characters in traditional narratives. Those aware of it turned defensive and apologetic, offering embarrassed explanations, curiously condemning carnality in biblical terms.

In the present day, the laws against same-sex intercourse and transgender behavior have remained unchanged—apparently because of apathy (suggested by the relatively few convictions over fifty years since independence compared to their widespread prevalence)—along with many other antiquated laws of the Indian penal code.

THE THIRD SEX AND GENDER IN INDIA

The people of the Indian continent, unlike their colonial masters, have always been exposed to a "third" gender—the "non-male, non-female" *napunsaka* (in Sanskrit) or *namard* (in Urdu). The terms are often used loosely to refer to a heterogeneous group, from homosexual cross-dressers to heterosexual transvestites, from transsexuals to transgendered individuals, every man who "does not do what men are supposed to do." Most are biologically male, often of homosexual or bisexual orientation, who live their social lives as women.

The reason for socially acknowledged gender metamorphosis varies from place to place. For example, in North Karnataka, a state in the southern half of India, male and female children are dedicated to the goddess Yellamma. These children are not allowed to marry or become members of mainstream society. They are expected to serve the goddess. As in folk belief, the goddess does not tolerate being touched by a man, the male children dedicated to her are forced to wear female apparel and adopt a female identity. These are the gender-variant male-priestesses known as *Jogappas,* who are also called the servants *(devadasis)* of Yellamma. They carry the image of the goddess on their head and travel from place to place offering blessings on behalf of the goddess and seeking alms. In the absence of economic support from the community, most devadasis of Yellamma end up as prostitutes and catamites.

Some male monks undergo gender metamorphosis and "become" women in their quest for liberation from the cycle of life. Those of the Shakta order believe that rejection of masculinity enables them to identify with the goddess Tripurasundari, the female manifestation of the supreme divine principle. The monks of the Vaishnava sakhibhava order, mentioned earlier, wear female apparel to earn divine grace by becoming the female companions or Sakhis of Radha, the beloved of Krishna, the supreme divine principle, the ultimate male.

By far the most common socially acknowledged third gender in India is the group known as *Hijras.* Unlike the Jogappas and the Sakhis, the Hijra is not just a third gender; it is also believed to be a third sex—neither male nor female. Not male, because they do not desire sexual relations with women. Not female, because they do not have a womb. Primarily biological males, rarely hermaphrodites, a few Hijra castrate themselves, as they have no use for the penis.

Scholars and activists, who tend to define Hijras as homosexual cross-dressers, transgendered individuals, eunuch transvestites, and male-to-female transsexuals, often overlook the fact that the Hijra are not simply a sexual orientation but also a well-defined social identity. To be Hijra, the crucial step is to take the vow of Hijrahood and become part of the Hijra clan, which almost functions as a caste with its own specific inner workings, rules, ritual, and hierarchy. Having accepted that one erotically desires members of the same sex and that one seeks to socialize as one of the opposite gender, one has to accept a senior Hijra as one's guru and join the guru's household or *gharana*. The guru initiates the novice into the Hijra way of life. This involves breaking all links with the heterosexual world and bowing to the will of the Hijra hierarchy. The male name is replaced by a female name in a symbolic rebirth. The novice adopts female attire and feminine mannerisms. He "becomes" a woman, almost. In the past, kings and noblemen were their patrons; they served in the royal inner apartments as caretakers and catamites. A few were given shelter in temples. Today, with the loss of royal and religious patronage, as they beg, sing, dance, bless, and curse for a living, the public treats them with a mixture of awe, dread, and disdain.

AN ANCIENT LEGACY

Is the modern-day Hijra a descendent of the ancient kliba? Scholars are not sure. It is generally believed that the practice of appointing eunuchs as guards in the seraglio came with central Asian Muslim warlords who invaded India around the twelfth century C.E. But there are similarities between the kliba and the Hijra. Similar to the Biblical injunction preventing those with mutilated genitals from entering the house of God, ancient Hindu law books prevented the kliba from becoming part of mainstream society. Likewise, since medieval times, the Hijras of India have lived separate lives, in the fringes of the heterosexual world, entertaining, begging, or prostituting themselves.

Most Indians believe that Hijras are born that way, that they are products of nature. The ancients believed this of the kliba too. The *Mahabharata* explains that the kliba is conceived when the white seed of man and the red seed of woman are of equal strength. Otherwise, if the father's seed is stronger, a male is conceived; if the mother's seed is stronger, a female is conceived. Since Hijras are not considered unnatural, it is easy to assimilate them in Indian society, though at the very fringes.

Many ancient cultures believed that the third sex is natural and carved out social roles for them. In *The Universal Myths*, Alexander Eliot narrates a tale from ancient Mesopotamia that explains why gods created eunuchs (probably a nonspecific term such as napunsaka/namard/kliba/Hijra referring to "non-men"). The wise watergod Enki created humans so that they could labor for the gods. In the celebration that followed, large quantities of beer were consumed. Enki's wife, the earth-goddess Ninmah, became light-headed and challenged Enki to give a purpose to humans whose bodies she sought to mutilate. She created a barren woman; Enki turned her into a concubine. She then created a eunuch; Enki turned him into a civil servant.

Arjuna, the hero of *Mahabharata* who loses his manhood for a year, serves as a dance teacher in the inner chambers of King Virtata, indicating that the practice of employing eunuchs in the royal women's quarters was prevalent in ancient India. The practice of using castrated males, who may or may not exhibit same-sex desire, as civil servants, dancers, singers, catamites, and palace guards was also prevalent in ancient Arabia, medieval Italy, and Imperial China. In fact, the eunuchs who served the emperors of ancient China had their own patron saint (Kang Ping Tieh), who castrated himself so that the emperor would not cast aspersions on his character as he served as regent in the Forbidden City, surrounded by royal concubines and eunuchs, while the emperor went out for a hunt.[12] Likewise, the Hijras of India have their own set of divine patrons. It is said that Hijras are specially favored by the goddess and have the power to bless or to curse. They are feared and held in awe. They are offered gifts during marriage and childbirth ceremonies. Barren women request them to dance and petition the goddess on their behalf. The close relationship between the goddess and the third sex/gender acquires greater significance in view of the fact that the castration is performed in the name of a folk goddess who in images is shown riding the Indian jungle fowl. The tale of this folk goddess, Baucharji-mata, whose temple is located in the state of Gujarat is retold in this book. Also retold is the tale of Khoothandavar, folk god from the southern state of Tamil Nadu, who accepts the Hijra, known as *Ali* in the South, as his lawfully wedded bride for one night.

WHAT ABOUT THE WOMEN?

The discerning reader will notice that women are hardly mentioned in the earlier discussion. Where is the sex-changing, gender-bending, same-sex desiring Hindu woman? If lesbians had a well-defined construct in traditional Hindu society, this is not very obvious from narrative traditions. There are more tales of male to female transformations than male to female transformations (biologically or socially) in Hindu lore. When a goddess takes on the traditional male role of warrior, she does not have to cross-dress; she marches into battle dressed in bridal finery. Even the third gender is dominated by biological males/social females. The concept of biological female/social male or the female-to-male transvestite/transsexual is not popular. Perhaps patriarchy silenced women who sought to oppose biological contours imposed by birth and erotic desires imposed by society. In Kerala, for example, a woman who behaved like a man (indicated by her attraction for women) was dismissed as an hysterical woman possessed by a Gandharva, a celestial spirit, who takes over the body of the mortal woman he found attractive.[13]

Interestingly, the androgynous divinity of Hinduism is seen as an aspect of a god, not a goddess. Also, every god in Hinduism depends on a feminine force known as shakti; goddesses do not have such a male counterpart. Images of male gods typically lack masculine musculature (so prominent in Greek art). Instead, they are sinuous and sensuous, almost like women. What does this preference for "feminine form" in a "patriarchal society" say about the Hindu attitude toward sex and gender, one wonders?

Images of women in erotic embrace are often found on temple walls and in miniature paintings. Are these to be seen as public acknowledgement of same-sex desire among women? It is difficult to answer this question as almost every Hindu scripture has been written by a male priest and almost every Hindu artwork is the work of a male artisan. In the Sanskrit epic *Valmiki Ramayana,* the women in the Rakshasa king Ravana's harem are described as making love to one another to taste the essence of their lord on one another's bodies. In a later day Purana, following the death of the king, two queens make love to each other to create a child. Both cases of lesbian sex, presented as poor substitutes to heterosexual intercourse, seem like clear cases of patriarchal voyeurism in my opinion.

Manusmriti lays down punishments for women having sex with other women, which indicates that lesbianism did exist in ancient India and was perceived as a problem by male law makers. According to the law-giver Manu (believed to be the first man and the harbinger of civilization in orthodox traditions), if a woman was caught having sex with a maiden, the maiden would be fined and whipped, while the woman would have her head shaved, her fingers cut off, and be made to ride on a donkey.[14]

REPRESENTATION IN NARRATIVES

The Hijras, the Jogappas, and even the Sakhis of India are known to indulge in same-sex activity. It is accepted as their way, even though some of them may have married women and fathered children. Perhaps the only way same-sex desire could express itself in traditional Hindu society was through sexual transformation and gender metamorphosis. Perhaps only by becoming a "woman" or by perceiving a man in feminine terms, was a man allowed to indulge homoerotic fantasies.

Anyone familiar with the traditional gay constructs in India will know that the penetrator/penetratee, active/passive, top/bottom, butch/femme divide dominates same-sex activity among men. The former is known as *panthi*, while the latter is known as *kothi*. The former retains his "masculine," even "straight," identity, while the latter forfeits it. A similar divide is seen in traditional gay constructs in many other parts of the world (e.g., Turkey, China, Arabia, Africa, Latin America) and was also reported in studies documenting MSM (men who have sex with men) activity in American prisons in the twentieth century.[15] Incidentally, the term *murath* or kothi is believed to have been appropriated from the Hijra construct by homosexuals living within the heterosexual construct. Could this socially tolerated heterosexual expression of homosexual desires be the reason why there are so many tales of sexual transformation and gender metamorphosis in Hindu lore?

Somewhere in the narrative vocabulary lurks a probable truth—that the transformations and metamorphoses serve as codes to voice desires that are unmentionable in a patriarchal, heterosexual world. Men who desire or behave like women, women who desire or behave like men, androgynes quivering for identity, in their quest to conform, have thus ended up in a womb-less, penis-less twilight zone where one is neither this nor that, or perhaps a bit of both. In a world where the philosophy tends to be polymorphous (accepting all possibilities), but where society tends to be dimorphous (dividing everything as masculine or feminine), all those who did not fit into one or the other compartment were bunched together in the category of the "compartment-less." Transvestites, transsexuals, impotent men,

men who had oral and anal sex, sterile men, hermaphrodites, eunuchs, homosexuals, sexually dysfunctional men, or all males who "did not do what men were supposed to do" were relegated into the vaguely defined, catchall phrase of "non-men" or "pseudo-women."

INTERPRETATION OF NARRATIVES

In the Hindu pantheon, many gods (such as the monkey-god *Hanuman* and the warrior-god *Ayyappa*) choose to remain celibate and prefer the company of men. No woman of fertile age, for example, is allowed to enter the temple of Ayyappa. At the same time there are many goddesses (such as Chinnamastika and Mahadevi) who have no male consorts, but are always surrounded by a band of rather aggressive and fearsome women known as *Yoginis, Dakinis, Matrikas,* and *Mahavidyas.* This has led a few writers to look upon these divinities in queer terms. These writers interpret a god's celibacy as "nonparticipation in reproductive sex," overlooking the pan-Indian belief in the spiritual and magical powers rising from retained semen. A goddess's virginity is perceived as "being unpenetrated," enabling the interpreter to look upon the goddess's companions as her lovers. Such "interpretations of convenience," often done in isolation without taking the entire Hindu worldview into consideration, though empowering to many in queer circles, can and do outrage most average and orthodox Hindus.

So when is an interpretation unacceptable? Is it unacceptable when it clashes with the orthodox viewpoint? For example, is it unacceptable to view Jonathan and David's friendship in sexual terms, simply because most Jewish scholars would not agree? Is it okay to consider homosexuality, rather than inhospitality, to be the crime of Sodom that brought down the wrath of Yahweh, simply because some Christian priests believe it to be so?

Every understanding of a symbol or lore, in my opinion, is ultimately an interpretation. All interpretations are subjective, colored and conditioned by the world one lives in. Retold in this book is the tale of the god Vishnu, preserver of the cosmos, who transforms into a nymph called Mohini and ends up sexually arousing the hermit-god Shiva. When this story was narrated in France, the members of the audience were quite taken by the "gay" plot. The narrator, an orthodox Hindu, was disturbed by their response. He found their interpretation "perverted." Years later, a friend asked me, "No Hindu that I know finds anything 'homosexual' in the tale. Why then did the French audience react so differently?" Why indeed? The only answer I could come up with was that maybe this was because the worldviews of the French audience and the Hindu narrator were radically different. The French audience, unfamiliar with tales of sexual transformation in their own sacred literature but quite familiar with nonheterosexual lifestyles in their society, had taken the tale literally. The Hindu narrator, familiar with the complex metaphorical nature of sacred Hindu lore but unfamiliar with nonheterosexual lifestyles, had preferred to view the tale along metaphysical lines.

We see what we want to see in a symbol. When Jews see the swastika, they remember Hitler and the Holocaust. When Hindus see the swastika, they think *"su-asti"* ("Let good things happen"). What has come to represent evil in one religion has for centuries symbolized auspiciousness in another. Writings of queer-unfriendly organizations suggest that in the Golden Age of the Hindu world (Krita Yuga) there was no queer activity, while writings of queer-friendly organizations see rejection of queer activity as a sign of the Dark Age (Kali Yuga). In my view, by limiting oneself to one interpretation one fails to see the big picture. Preference for one interpretation does not invalidate other viewpoints. This truism has been kept in mind while writing this book.

STRUCTURE AND AIM OF THE BOOK

The stories in this book are not reproductions, translations, or transliteration; they are *my* retellings that bring together the idea dominating the several versions of the narrative. Some of the stories retold are not queer (the story of Narasimha in Chapter 5, for example), but they help make the queer plots and characters more comprehensible. Most of the stories have been taken from the classical tradition (Sanskrit scriptures) of Hinduism. Some have been taken from the folk tradition (vernacular narratives, both oral and written). A few come from Buddhist, Jain, and Thai sources that share many beliefs with the Hindus.

Chapter 1 deals with female-to-male transformation that enables women to take up traditional male roles. Chapters 2 and 3 both deal with male-to-female transformation. Narratives rarely make it clear whether the transformation is biological or cosmetic (cross-dressing). Chapter 2 discusses the former variety of tales where transformed men either forget their male essence or experience a female biological process such as pregnancy. This is usually the result of a curse or an accident. In Chapter 3, despite change in gender, the character remains aware of his male essence, suggesting that the transformation is merely a cross-dressing subterfuge. Chapter 4 brings together tales associated with castration. In Chapter 5, the issue of divine androgyny is explored in the context of masculine and feminine roles and symbols in Hindu occult, mystical, philosophical, and ritual culture.

As the tales are retold, I inform the reader how I came upon each narrative. I then try to explain their presence in the context of dominant Hindu attitudes toward sex, gender, pleasure, fertility, and celibacy. Many may not agree with the stands I take or the interpretations I make. That is okay; everyone sees the world through a different pair of eyes. As I always say:

> Within infinite myths lies the Eternal Truth,
>
> Who sees it all?
>
> Varuna has but a thousand eyes
>
> Indra has a hundred
>
> And I, only two[16]

It is possible that there are many other queer stories out there of which I am not aware. Hopefully, someone will compile them and publish them later. The purpose of writing this book is simple: to spread awareness of tales that are otherwise hush-hush in a world uncomfortable with the queer aspects of its culture. I hope you find them entertaining and enlightening.

Chapter 1

Women Who Become Men

Shikhandi is a minor but pivotal character in the Hindu epic *Mahabharata*. His/her ambiguous sexuality has confounded story-tellers, playwrights, and filmmakers for generations. In 1988, in a mega-teleserial called *Mahabharata* produced by B. R. Chopra and telecast by Doordarshan (India's state-owned television broadcasting service), the role of Shikhandi was played by a male actor who walked with an exaggerated feminine gait, his entry accompanied by a sinister background music. In Ramanand Sagar's teleserial *Shree Krishna,* telecast a few years later, the role was played by a female actor sporting a moustache. Renowned playwright Peter Brook also used a woman to portray Shikhandi in his internationally acclaimed play *Le Mahabharata*. Shikhandi is neither male nor female. Or rather, Shikhandi is both male and female. A woman in her/his former life, she/he is born with a female body, but is raised as a man. Though she/he acquires a male body on her/his wedding night, in the climax of her/his life, she/he is treated as a woman.

A man with a woman's heart? A woman with a man's body? A hermaphrodite? A Hijra? Nobody is sure, yet the term "Shikhandi" continues to be used in common parlance in a derogatory manner to refer to an effeminate man or a masculine woman. This is often done without knowledge of the details of Shikhandi's life that are edited out of most abridged and popular versions of the *Mahabharata*. For example, in Iravati Karve's *Yuganta,* the now legendary commentary on the great epic, the author describes Shikhandi as a man who in his last life was a woman called Amba. This detail is well known as it plays a crucial part in the unfolding of the narrative. The same line of thought is expressed in Kamala Subramaniam's *Mahabharata*. What is left unsaid is that Amba was reborn with the body of a woman, but was raised as a man by her father. What is also left unsaid is how the female body transformed into a male body.

To understand Shikhandi, we must learn more about Amba. To learn about Amba—and her tragedy in a man's world—we have to make our way through a labyrinth of plots and search the multitude of personalities who populate the epic, until we stumble upon a character called Bhisma. Before narrating the story of Bhisma and how he is related to Amba and how Amba becomes Shikhandi, let us take a closer look at *Mahabharata* itself.

Mahabharata is an epic written in Sanskrit (Hindu equivalent of Latin) verse that is nearly eight times larger than the *Iliad* and *Odyssey* put together. It reached its final form somewhere between 300 B.C.E. and 300 C.E., the period that saw the rise and fall of the Classical Roman Empire. It is generally accepted that the epic was originally a smaller simpler folk story. Over time, it was appropriated, "sanskritized," and sanitized by Brahmins, the priestly caste that has dominated the traditional Hindu caste hierarchy for over 3,000 years. The plot revolves only around priests and their patrons, kings, and warriors, while common folk—such as traders, farmers, herdsmen, and craftsmen—are reduced to narrative props. Earlier the book was known as *Jaya* (meaning "victory") and comprised of a few thousand verses. Later, as the tale moved from the tongues of wandering minstrels into the libraries of priests, it was embellished with the genealogies of kings and other didactic material such as cosmogonies, cosmologies, philosophies, and astrological forecasts.

The present version, called *Mahabharata* (Maha means "great"; bharata is both the traditional name of India as well as an ancient line of kings), includes eighteen chapters and spans over seven generations of Bharata kings, beginning with Pratipa, Bhisma's grandfather, and ending with Janamajeya, Bhisma's great-great-grandson. At the heart of the narrative is the struggle between the Pandavas and their cousins, the Kauravas, for the throne of Hastinapur, which culminates in a terrible war on the battlefield of Kurukshetra.

Most Hindus do not consider *Mahabharata* to be a work of fiction. It is treated as *itihasa*, or history. Some may call it legendary history based on a real fratricidal struggle that took place around 1000 B.C.E., about the time it is believed Solomon built his temple in Jerusalem and the Myceneans attacked the city of Troy. Traditional dating systems push back the date of war to around 3000 B.C.E. Vyasa, the legendary compiler of the Vedic scriptures, is believed to be the author of the epic. Ganapati, the elephant-headed god of beginnings, served as his scribe. This makes *Mahabharata* a religious scripture. It also acquires the status of a sacred book because one of its characters is Krishna, believed by many to be the Supreme Personality of Godhead. More about him and his divine discourse the *Bhagavad Gita* will be discussed later. Let us focus on Bhimsa first.

BHISMA: THE SON WHO SWORE CELIBACY

The river-nymph Ganga agreed to marry Shantanu, King of Hastinapur and Lord of the Kuru clan, only if he swore never to question her actions after marriage. Blinded by desire, Shantanu agreed. He was, as a result, forced to remain silent when Ganga drowned their seven sons as soon as she gave birth to them (to liberate them from a curse). When Ganga was about to kill the eighth child, Shantanu could remain silent no more. He spoke up, stopped her, saved the newborn, but lost the river-nymph's affection forever. The eighth son was named Devavrata, who grew up to be a skilled archer and a worthy crown prince greatly loved by the people. Then, one day, Shantanu fell in love with a fisherwoman called Satyavati, who agreed to marry him only if he promised to make her children his heirs. Shantanu hesitated until Devavrata came to his aid and gave up his claim to the throne. This did not satisfy Satyavati. "What if Devavrata's children fight my children for a share of the kingdom?" To put her mind to rest, Devavrata took a vow: "I will take no woman to my bed and so never father children." For this act of filial affection, the gods blessed Devavrata and renamed him Bhisma, the awesome one.

The renaming of Devavrata to Bhisma after he took the vow of celibacy makes one wonder what is so awesome about not fathering a child. In Jain retellings of the *Mahabharata,* it is said that to leave no doubt in the mind of Satyavati, Devavrata performed the awesome act of castrating himself.[1] This detail is not found in Hindu retellings of the epic. The answer to the renaming probably lies in the Hindu belief in the cycle of rebirth. In the Hindu scheme of things, every man is indebted to his ancestors, the venerable *Pitrs,* for his existence. He repays his debt by fathering children and facilitating their rebirth. A son is called *put-ra* and a daughter *put-ri* because their birth saves fathers from the dreaded realm known as Put, reserved for childless men. The Pitrs hang over the precipice of oblivion in the land of the dead until a living descendent comes to their rescue. During the ceremony of *shraadh*, devout Hindus make offerings of rice balls to their forefathers and promise to fulfill their biological obligation. By refusing to father children, Devavrata incurs the wrath of his ancestors and condemns himself to an eternity in the land of the dead. Sacrificing his very existence for the sake of his father earns him the admiration of the gods and transforms him into Bhisma. The admiration for Bhisma is so great that every year on the eight day of the waxing moon in the month of Magha (late January or early February), the day Bhisma is said to have died, devout Hindus perform funerary rites in Bhisma's name and offer rice balls to the eternally suffering, childless son of Shantanu, to assuage his interminable hunger.

The tale of Bhisma is a reminder of the fate of a childless man in the Hindu worldview. It is also the tale of the ideal Hindu son: he who subsumes personal desire to please his father. The following story from the *Markandeya Purana* (c. 250 C.E.) is the tale of another such ideal son. It is retold by Sadashiv Ambadas Dange in his *Encyclopaedia of Puranic Beliefs and Practices,* Volume I.

AVIKSHITA: THE PRINCE WHO BELIEVED HE WAS A WOMAN

Many women wanted to marry Avikshita, son of King Karandhama, but he turned them down because he believed himself to be a woman. When he rejected Princess Vaishalini, she decided to kill herself, but was stopped by a celestial being who foretold that she would be the mother of a great king. She went to the forest and decided to perform austerities until circumstances changed in her favor. Avikshita's mother, Vira, began a fast and observed a vow to get what she desired most (the marriage of her son). Meanwhile, Avikshita— on the way to the forest—gallantly declared that before leaving he would fulfill the wishes of anyone who approached him. His father, the king, went to him and said, "Fulfill my wish. Give me a grandson." While wandering in the forest, Avikshita heard a woman cry out for help as she was being abducted by a demon. He rushed to her rescue. The woman was Vaishalini, who eventually bore his son, Marutta.

Avikshita believes himself to be a woman. Nevertheless, his mother wants him to marry and his father wants him to produce a child. Even the woman who wants to marry him is unconcerned about his self-identification. Ultimately, probably under societal pressure (though the narrative does not make this clear), Avikshita gets married. Similar to Bhisma, Avikshita is the selfless son, much desired by Hindu families. For the sake of his father, Bhisma does not marry. For the sake of his father, Avikshita does marry. Personal desires are crushed on the altar of filial duty.

Mahabharata informs us of another such ideal son, Prince Puru (Bhisma's ancestor), who endures his father's old age so that his father can continue enjoying the joys of youth. For this action, the father makes Puru his heir, even though he is born of a concubine and is the youngest of four sons.

Admiration for a man who sacrifices his pleasures for the sake of his father has been described by some Indian psychoanalysts as "reverse-Oedipus" complex.[2] Unlike the Freudian model based on Greek myths where the son kills the father who he perceived as a sexual rival, in the Indian model, it is the father who overpowers his sexual rival, the son.

Getting back to Bhisma, even though he turns away from women, circumstances entwine his life with the life of Amba, the princess of Kashi, the woman who ultimately becomes his nemesis.

AMBA'S QUEST FOR MANHOOD

Satyavati had two sons by Shantanu. The first, Chitrangada, was killed in war before he could marry and father children. The second, Vichitravirya, was so weak that he could not find himself a bride. So, on his behalf, in keeping with the ancient code of marriage, Bhisma—now patriarch of the Kuru clan, abducted the three daughters of the king of Kashi and brought them to Hastinapur. Two of the three princesses, Ambika and Ambalika, agreed to marry Vichitravirya. The eldest one, Amba, wished to marry the man she was in love with. Content with two wives, Vichitravirya let Amba go to her beloved. Unfortunately, Amba's lover refused to accept her as she had been "touched by another man." Desperate, Amba sought shelter in Hastinapur. Vichitravirya refused to take back "that which is once given away." Destitute, she begged Bhisma, who she blamed for her misfortune, to marry her. When Bhisma refused, Amba decided to use force to make him change his mind. She sought a champion who would fight, defeat, and compel Bhisma to marry her. Failing to find one, she invoked Shiva, lord of destruction. Shiva promised her that in her next life she would be the cause of Bhisma's death. Impatient to kill Bhisma, Amba killed herself and made a hasty journey to her next life.

Vyasa portrays Bhisma as a tragic figure. He abandons family life, but family life does not abandon him. He is a bachelor by choice but a householder by obligation. The early death of his father forces Bhisma to become the head of a household, become regent, and take care of the women and children. He is forced to become a patriarch, despite his great vow of renunciation. He rejects the traditional key to worldly life, marriage, but ends up a worldly man nevertheless. In many ways he is a non-son: he does not marry, he does not continue his father's lineage, he does not inherit his father's crown, and ultimately, he dies at the hands of one who is not a man, a shameful fate for a proud warrior.

In the world that is *Mahabharata,* things are different for men and women. While Bhisma takes his decision, decisions are taken for Amba. Her abduction at the hands of Bhisma deprives her of the right to choose her husband (this ceremony where women chose their husbands from a gathering of men known as *swayamvara* died out in ancient India with the rise of patriarchy). Her father, the king of Kashi, refuses to take any responsibility for her once she has crossed his threshold, never mind that she is carried over by force by a man who gives her away, like a gift, to his younger brother. Her lover rejects her because "she is touched by another." Vichitravirya refuses to take her back because "gifts once given cannot be taken back." Bhisma refuses to accept responsibility for Amba's misfortune. When she seeks justice by force, social laws prevent her from taking up arms; she needs a champion to fight her case. When she fails to find a suitable champion, she does not give up. Determined to have her revenge, she kills herself and hopes to be reborn as a man, thus acquiring the biology that earns her the right to bear weapons.

What happens between Amba's death and rebirth? The following story concerns Bhisma's half-brother, Vichitravirya, scion of the Kuru clan, whose name can be translated as "queer virility" or "odd semen" (in Sanskrit, *vichitra* = odd, *virya* = semen, manliness, virility).

CHILDREN OF THE MAN WITH QUEER VIRILITY

Vichitravirya died before he could make either of his wives pregnant, so Satyavati asked Bhisma to go to the widows and give them children. He refused, reminding her of his vow. Desperate, Satyavati sent for a sage who impregnated the two queens. Ambika gave birth to Dhritarashtra, while Ambalika gave birth to Pandu. Dhritarashtra was born blind. His physically imperfection denied him kingship. He married Gandhari and fathered the hundred Kauravas. During a hunt, Pandu accidentally killed a sage and his wife while they were making love. Before dying, the sage cursed him, "If you ever touch your wife you will die." The curse prevented him from impregnating his two wives, and Pandu gave up his crown. He appointed Dhritarashtra regent and retired to the forest, considering himself unworthy of kingship. Pandu's wives found a solution to this situation, however. They invoked the celestial Devas, who gave them five sons, who came to be known as the Pandavas, the sons of Pandu. The two branches of the Kuru clan, the Kauravas and Pandavas, grew up hating each other, each one believing they had a greater claim to the throne of Hastinapur, much to the chagrin of their great-grandmother Satyavati.

There is poetic justice in this narrative. Satyavati prevents Bhisma from fathering children in order to secure her children's hold on the crown. What she does not anticipate is that her own progeny will end up fighting over the crown. Thus, the *Mahabharata* captures the grand Hindu discourse on destiny: no matter how hard man may seek to manipulate destiny, he will always fail. No human can fathom the mysterious workings of karma.

Traditionally, a direct relationship is believed to exist between potency of semen and strength of body. An impotent/sterile man is considered to be a physically weak man, and a physically weak man is considered to be an impotent/sterile man. Thus, there may be a link between Vichitravirya's name, his dependence on his half-brother Bhisma to get him a wife, his inability to father a child, and his early death. Though functionally male, he is effectively a non-man, because he does not impregnate either wife.

In Jain retellings,[3] Dhritarashtra's physical defect (blindness) extends to his sexual prowess: he is said to be sterile. In desperation, his wife Gandhari, who shares his blindness as a dutiful wife by blindfolding herself, copulates with one hundred billy goats. The goats are sacrificed to the gods by Dhritarashtra in his quest to father children. The slaughtered goats, who are reborn as celestial beings, visit Gandhari, one who loved them in her last life, and give her one hundred sons.

The story alludes to the practice of niyoga or levirate, which enables Pandu—rendered functionally impotent by a curse—to father sons. Niyoga was a ritually prescribed course of action open to all men who could not beget children on their own: they could let any other man, a relative or a sage preferably, to cohabit with their wife/wives. The children conceived belonged to the lawfully married husband, even after his death. This practice enabled non-men to father children and escape the fate of being childless men. One might speculate that this was the option given to homosexual men who could not or did not have intercourse with their wives. This ensured that all men, irrespective of their sexual orientation, could fulfill their social roles (marry) and gender obligations (reproduce).

Children were required for reasons other than satisfying the ancestors. Drupada, the king of Panchala, Amba's father in her next life, wanted a child who would avenge his humiliation at the hands of the Brahmin Drona. The Brahmin Drona and Prince Drupada were childhood friends who had sworn to share their worldly fortunes with each other. Years later, Drona, reduced to poverty, approached Drupada, who has risen to be King of Panchala, and sought wealth in memory of the childhood pact. "Friendship exists only between equals," Drupada said disparagingly, "Ask for money therefore in charity, not friendship." Hurt by this remark, Drona decided to teach Drupada a lesson. He learned the art of war, gained employment in Hastinapur under Bhisma, taught the Kuru princes the martial arts, and demanded as fee one half of Drupada's kingdom. The princes obliged, thus enabling Drona to become their equal. Humiliated by the course of events, Drupada invoked Shiva, the god of destruction, and sought a son who would kill the Brahmin Drona and avenge his defeat.

SHIKHANDINI GETS A MALE BODY

Drupada's wife gave birth to a daughter. Refusing to accept that Shiva would lie to him, Drupada decided to raise his daughter as a man. The girl, named Shikhandini, was taught all the skills reserved for men. She grew up believing she was a man. She was even given a wife. But on the wedding night, when the bride discovered that her husband was a woman, she ran to her father in a state of shock. Determined to avenge this insult, the bride's father, King Hiranyavarna of Dasarna, raised an army and threatened to invade Panchala. Drupada knew that the only way to save his kingdom was to prove that his "son" was truly a man. He also knew that this was impossible. Confronted with her femininity for the first time in her life, Shikhandini felt responsible for this calamity. Resolving to kill herself, she went to the forest and happened upon a yaksha called Sthuna. This forest spirit felt sorry for Shikhandini and offered to exchange his sex with her for one night. Shikhandini accepted the offer, took the yaksha's manhood, and returned to Panchala where she proclaimed she was ready to prove her masculinity to anyone who cared to test it. Hiranyavarna sent his courtesans, who sent back a satisfactory report. Concluding that his daughter had made a mistake, Hiranyavarna apologized to Drupada and sent his daughter back. Shikhandini, now a man called Shikhandi, performed his husbandly duties to the satisfaction of his newly wedded wife. In the meanwhile, the obliging yaksha was punished by his overlord Kubera for changing his sex and was condemned to retain the female sex he had assumed. When Shikhandi, true to his promise, came to the yaksha to return his borrowed male sex, Kubera was so pleased with his honesty that he allowed Shikhandi to remain a male as long as he lived. And because the yaksha had surrendered his sex in a worthy cause, Kubera decreed that he would get back his male sex as soon as Shikhandi died.

In their quest for vengeance, both Amba and Drupada invoke Shiva. Not only is Shiva the god of destruction, he is also the only god who breaks free from the rigid orthodox scheme of things. He transcends the conventional, kills even those who cannot be killed. He is associated with Brahmahatya, the act of killing a Brahmin or Hindu priest, which is the greatest ritual crime in Hinduism. The *Shiva Purana* (c. 750 to 1350 C.E.) states that Shiva was the only one to not shy away from beheading Brahma, the god of creation, the primal priest, when the latter made love to his daughter, the primal woman. Only through the grace of Shiva, Drupada believes, can he father a child who will disregard the mantle of ritual protection and kill the Brahmin Drona. Likewise, Amba believes, that only through the grace of

Shiva can she kill Bhisma, the man who has been blessed by the gods to choose the circumstances and the time of his death.

The sexual transformation of Shikhandini to Shikhandi is a motif common in many Indian folk tales that deal with female to male transformation. A yaksha is a forest spirit who is closely associated with Shiva. Yaksha are keepers of secret wealth and may be seen as Indian counterparts of the European "faerie" (Kubera being the Hindu incarnation of Shakespeare's Oberon). They are plump, short, often deformed, and associated with money and magic. In folk tales, the role of the yaksha is sometimes taken up either by a sorcerer, ghosts, or a village god. The following North Indian folk tale is retold in Randolph and colleagues', *Cassell's Encyclopedia of Queer Myth, Symbol, and Spirit*.

THE RAJA'S DAUGHTER WHO BECAME HIS SON

A Hindu king refused to send his daughter to the seraglio of his feudal overlord, the Sultan of Delhi, as custom dictated. When the sultan's army was sent to bring the kings daughter by force, the girl took refuge in the temple of a goddess. The sultan had the door of the temple broken. Once inside, to his greatest surprise, he discovered that the girl had turned into a boy. Losing interest, he returned to Delhi. The king was so overjoyed and grateful that he had many temples built in honor of the goddess.

This story can be dated to after the invasion of India by Central Asian warlords and the establishment of the Delhi Sultanate around the twelfth century C.E, at least a thousand years after the *Mahabharata* reached its final form. The period that followed is considered a time of great social upheaval. The new rulers of the land, whose worldview—forcefully imposed—differed greatly from the natives, threatened the Hindu sociocultural fabric. In the previous narrative, the honor of the princess, and by extension, that of her father's family, is protected when the goddess changes the sex of the child. The king is grateful for this.

In another story retold by Giti Thadani in her book *Sakhiyani*, sexual transformation brings sorrow, not joy. Based on a Rajasthani folk tale, this story was the subject of a short Hindi story by Vijay Dan Detha, which has been translated and compiled in the book *Same-Sex Love in India*. It inspired a play *Beeja-Teeja* in the 1970s. This story, with its feminist undertones, is most certainly a radical modern-day reworking of a medieval narrative in which, in all probability, sexual transformation satisfied the traditional heterosexual and patriarchal paradigm. It is interesting to note that the name for the woman who becomes a man is Beeja, "beej" meaning seed. The name for the woman who remains a woman is Teeja, "teej" referring to a vow kept by women for the welfare of husbands. The story may challenge traditional attitude toward sexuality, but the names evoke traditional roles.

THE GIRLS WHO GOT MARRIED

Two friends met at a fair. When they discovered that each one's wife was pregnant, they decided to seal their friendship through the marriage of the unborn children. The ceremony was hastily performed. Unfortunately, both children turned out to be females—Teeja and Beeja. The marriage would have been annulled, but Beeja's father decided to keep his daughter's womanhood a secret, probably because he eyed the dowry. Beeja was raised a boy. Villagers who knew about the deception kept quiet. Eventually, Beeja married Teeja. On their wedding night, Teeja discovered the truth. She was not angry. Instead, she suggested Beeja dress up in female apparel since she was a woman. The villagers tolerated Beeja living with Teeja as long as she wore male attire, but were furious when they saw Beeja in female attire. They drove the two girls out of the village. As they left, Teeja and Beeja made a scarecrow to tell villagers what they thought of them. In the forest, the two girls came upon an abandoned well in the forest that was inhabited by ghosts. "Aren't you scared of us?" asked the ghosts. "No, we are not. We fear humans more," said the girls. For some time, the two girls lived happily with the ghosts in the well. The ghosts even built them a house. Then, succumbing to Teeja's desperation to reintegrate with society, Beeja agreed to become a man. The ghosts used their magic powers and did the needful. Dressed in male attire, Beeja returned to the village with his wife. The villagers did not turn them away. As the days passed, Teeja noticed a change in Beeja's personality. Beeja began abusing Teeja, hitting her if he found her wanting in her wifely duties. Unhappy, Teeja ran into the forest. When Beeja tried to bring her back, she cried, "You were nicer when you were a woman." To restore their love and marriage, Beeja asked the ghosts to turn her back into a woman and the two girls lived happily ever after in the forest with the ghosts in the well.

In folk Hinduism, when a woman dies violently before she can become a wife or mother, it is believed that she comes back to haunt those responsible for her death. To appease her hostile spirit, she comes to be identified with the village goddess or Grama-devis. These Grama-devis, or Mata-jis, are held responsible for droughts, epidemics, miscarriages, and lethal childhood fevers. Their shrines are nothing more than vermilion smeared rocks located in river backs and crossroads, occasionally topped with brass masks and enclosed in a shrine. They are remembered only when calamity strikes a village or a family. Grama-devis are appeased with gifts of sweets and bridal finery.[4] When I read the story of Teeja and Beeja in Giti Thadani's book, I thought of all those stories reported in Indian newspapers of lesbian couples who kill themselves in suicide pacts when their families stop them from seeing each other.[5, 6] And then, I thought of the twin goddesses worshipped in different parts of India: Chamunda and Chotila in Gujarat,[7] Chamunda and Keliama in Uttar Pradesh, and Durgamma and Dayamava in Karnataka. Could it be that the twin-goddess shrines of India are shrines built in memory of women who loved each other and killed themselves rather than suffer the brutality of a homophobic society? Could they be manifestations of soul mates, the *jami* twins, that Giti Thadani talks about in her book *Sakhiyani?*

My attempts to get more information on the twin goddesses have not yielded many results. Legends of folk gods and goddesses are usually passed down orally and often cannot be corraborated. In Pupul Jayakar's book *Earth Mother*, there is the story of Durgamma and Dayamava. Durgamma, a high-caste Brahmin girl, is duped into marrying a low-caste cobbler who poses as a scholar and a priest. When she discovers the truth, she raises a sickle and kills her husband. Each year, a festival is held to commemorate the event. The husband—represented by a male buffalo—is sacrificed and the goddess goes through ritual widowhood. The villagers walk on fire, swing on hooks, and pierce their tongues with nails in a kind of ritual atonement. This is no doubt a fertility festival, where the blood and violence restores the fecundity of the soil after harvest. But the narrative associated with the ritual does not explain the consort-like presence of the second goddess beside the primary deity. Identified as Durgamma's sister, friend, or companion, Dayamava is treated with indifference. Maybe the tale of the twin goddesses died with the original builders of the shrine. Of course, there can be several alternative explanations for the twinning. They could be, as suggested in Wendy Doniger's book (and cover) *Splitting the Difference,* the goddess and her less perfect, more human, shadow-twin.

Nevertheless, there are holy places associated with two inseparable women such as the Shudri-Brahamani-tirtha. The tale associated with this holy place can be found in Sadashiv Ambadas Dange's *Encyclopaedia of Puranic Beliefs and Practices,* Volume III. It comes from the *Skanda Purana* (700 to 1150 C.E.). Note the presence of Shiva, the destroyer, the god who breaks free of all conventions.

THE INSEPARABLE GIRLS

Ratnavali, daughter of the Shudra king of Anarta, and Brahmani, daughter of the priest of Anarta, were the best of friends. They could not bear the thought of being separated after marriage. They preferred death. On learning of the intensity of their emotion, the king decided that the two girls should be given in marriage to the same household—Ratnavali would marry the king and Brahmani would marry the resident priest. A proposal was sent to King Brihadbala of Dasharna, who accepted it and set out for Anarta. Meanwhile, a youth in Anarta visited a prostitute and consumed wine. To wash away the sin, he had the choice of drinking scalding hot butter or touching the breasts of a virgin princess, thinking of her as his mother. The youth's parents begged the king of Anarta to let their son touch his daughter, as the other recommended method for expiation was lethal. The king relented and the youth touched Ratnavali's breasts. Ratnavali was told to look upon the youth as her son. Instantly, her breasts oozed milk. When the news spread, King Brihadbala of Dasharna turned back because he believed his betrothed to be tainted. Brahmani could not marry either because she had waited for sixteen years for Ratnavali to marry and was now too old to be a bride. The two unmarried girls left their parents' houses, sought refuge in the forest near a water tank, and performed penance under guidance of sage Bhartryagna. Shiva appeared before Brahmani and blessed her. Brahmani refused to take the blessing until

Shiva appeared before Ratnavali and blessed her too. The place where Shiva blessed the two girls became a holy place known as Shudri-Brahmani-tirtha.

The parents of the two girls do not consider their affection for each other a hindrance to marriage. Room is made for personal desire (same-sex love) as well a social duty (marriage within caste rules). Circumstances, however, do not support the latter and the girls are left to fend for themselves.

Returning to the tale of Shikhandi. She/he was destined to kill Bhisma, the patriarch of the Kuru clan, not its preceptor, Drona, as Drupada discovered to his disappointment. One day, Shikhandi hung around his neck a garland that for years had been hanging on the gateway of Drupada's court. It was foretold that whosoever placed the garland around his neck would kill Bhisma. Realizing that Shikhandi was not quite the son he wanted, Drupada performed a *yagna,* a Vedic ceremony that invokes and appeases celestial spirits known as Devas. The ritual yielded a magic potion that would create such a child. The sages and priests sent for Drupada's wife, but when she did not arrive at the appointed hour, they poured the potion into the fire altar. From the flames emerged a fully grown man and woman. The man, Dhristdhyumna, it was foretold, would kill Drona while the woman, Draupadi, would marry the Pandavas and be responsible for the destruction of the Kauravas.

Children born of Shiva's grace turn out androgynous. Shikhandi is born with a female body and ends up with a male body. The second child would have been androgynous, too, but the sages poured the child-conceiving magic potion into the fire and it split into a male and a female child. Dhristadhyumna is a ferocious warrior who does not shy away from killing a Brahmin. Draupadi is a dark and voluptuous woman, so alluring that every man wanted to be her lover and every woman who saw her wanted to turn into a man so as to make love to her.[8] He is the manly male. She is the womanly female. Between them stands Shikhandi, the manly female.

Details of Amba's life as a girl raised as a boy cannot be found in any retelling of the *Mahabharata.* One wonders, then, how would she have reacted when she discovered her genitals were different from those of other boys? Freud would have had a field day psychoanalyzing her. Would she have developed a castration complex? Would she have treated her father as a competitor for her mother's affection? Would she have seen her mother as a competitor? How did she react to her younger siblings—Draupadi, the daughter who was raised as a girl, and Dhristadhyumna, the son who was raised as a boy? The narrative does not explore the relationship between the two sisters, the masculine Shikhandini and the feminine Draupadi. We are never told if Shikhandi envies Draupadi's trousseau or if Draupadi envies Shikhandini's right to bear arms. We are also not told of how Shikhandi treats her younger brother who had male genitals. In my opinion, a great chance to explore the mind of the characters was overlooked. Perhaps the complexities of sexuality overwhelmed Vyasa, or perhaps episodes that made embarrassing reading were simply edited away by future generations. We will never know.

Shikhandi is raised as a man and later acquires a male body, but not everyone looks upon him as a man. This irony is based on the climax of Shikhandi's life, on the battlefield of Kurukshetra.

MAN WHO WAS A WOMAN

The Pandavas and the Kauravas, though cousins, hated each other, each one believing that they had a greater claim to the throne of Hastinapur. To bring peace, the kingdom was divided and the underdeveloped half given to the Pandavas who, with the aid of their friend and benefactor Krishna, transformed it into a rich and prosperous land called Indraprastha. Envious of their success, the Kauravas invited the Pandavas to a game of dice and manipulated them into gambling away their rights to Indraprastha for thirteen years. After the stipulated period had passed, the Kauravas refused to return Indraprastha to the Pandavas. This led to a war. The Pandavas were determined to use force to regain their kingdom, which the Kauravas had obtained through trickery. But when the two armies met on the plains of Kurukshetra, the grand old sire Bhisma, who led the Kaurava army, kept the Pandava force in check for nine days. The Pandavas learned that Bhisma could not be defeated as long as he held his bow in hand and that he never lowered his bow before a man. "So let us bring before him a man who is not quite a man. Let Shikhandi confront him tomorrow," said Krishna. On the tenth day of the war, Shikhandi rode into battle on Arjuna's chariot, acting as his human shield. Bhisma took one look at Shikhandi, the man who was woman in his past life and was born with a female body in his present life, and lowered his bow. At that very moment,

Arjuna shot arrows at Bhisma, driving so many of them into his body that there was not a space of two fingers left on him that was without a wound. Later, in a night raid, Ashvathama, son of Drona, killed Shikhandi by cutting his body in half.

After the arrows pierce his body, Bhisma does not die instantly. He has the gift of choosing the time of his death and he chooses to die only after the winter solstice, when the sun begins its northern journey along the horizon, known to Hindus as *uttarayana*. In Hindu cosmology, the year is divided into two halves: the bright half from the winter solstice to the summer solstice when the gods rise to rule the cosmos and the dark half from the summer solstice to the winter solstice when the ancestors, the Pitrs, are in control. Perhaps Bhisma, the childless man, did not want to face his ancestors. So, he chose to die only after the winter solstice when his forefathers had returned to the land of the dead. Until then, he lay on a bed of arrows watching the collapse of the old order and the rise of the new in a bloody struggle for power on the battlefield of Kurushetra.

Bhisma declares several times during the war that he will never fight or kill a woman, anyone who used to be a woman (transsexual?), has a woman's name, or appears to be a woman (cross-dresser or transvestite?). Does this mean Bhisma respects women? Or does it mean women are too lowly to fight? When the river-nymph Ganga hears that her son Bhisma had died at the hands of a woman, she is heartbroken. "How can he who could defeat all the kings of the world when he abducted the princess of Kashi, fall to a woman?" she asks. She is consoled only when she hears the details: that a man (Arjuna) not a non-man (Shikhandi) shot the fatal arrows.

Krishna treats Shikhandi as a man, inviting him to ride with Arjuna into battle. Bhisma, however, views Shikhandi as a woman, a view that leads to his death. Obviously, the change in biology makes no difference to Bhisma. So how then does one define identity, if not by biology? That is the question raised by the story of Shikhandi. In her book *The World of Homosexuals,* Shakuntala Devi interviewed an old Tamil priest who explained homosexuality as resulting from a female soul trapped in a male body, or a male soul trapped in a female body.[9] Belief in sexual souls (or probably life-breaths with gender identity) forms the foundation of a Sanskrit play in which the god of death accidentally exchanges the soul of a courtesan with the soul of a priest. As a result, the priest starts behaving as a courtesan while the courtesan starts behaving as a priest.[10] Perhaps Shikhandi had a female soul, or at least a female essence, and that made her a woman, according to Bhisma. Krishna, however, gave Shikhandi's biology greater importance.

How did Shikhandi perceive himself/herself? As a woman wronged by Bhisma? As a man who married the daughter of Hiranayavarna? As a female warrior who Bhisma refused to fight? As a male warrior who faced other Kaurava warriors in battle before meeting his death at the hands of Ashvathama? That is a question the *Mahabharata* does not answer.

The question may be raised, "Why does Amba need to become a man to avenge herself?" Before answering this question, let us take a look at the following story from the *Yogavasistha-Maha Ramayana* (c. 1000 C.E.). The story is retold in Wendy Doniger's *Splitting the Difference*.

THE WOMAN WHO BECAME A MAN AND THEN A WOMAN

King Shikhidhvaja loved his wife Cudala very much, though he never gave her much credit for her wisdom. Unknown to him, she was an extremely enlightened woman with many magical powers including the ability to change her form. One day, the king decided to renounce his kingdom and go to the forest in search of true knowledge. He refused to take his wife along. She stayed back to govern the kingdom. Eighteen years later, Cudala paid her husband a visit, taking the form of a young priest called Kumbhaka. Shikhidhvaja and Kumbhaka became great friends. Kumbhaka shared his knowledge with Shikhidhvaja who was very receptive to his wise words. Kumbhaka felt desire for Shikhidhvaja and wondered how they could make love without him having to reveal his identity. He came up with a plan. He told the king, "I saw the hot-tempered sage Durvasa hurrying through the sky and remarked that he looked like a woman running to meet her lover. The sage did not take this comment kindly and cursed me that I would turn into a woman every night." That night, in front of the king, Kumbhaka turned into a woman called Madanika. The king let Madanika sleep in his hermitage but made no attempts to have sex with her. Every day, the king would listen to the wise words of Kumbhaka and every night he would sleep dispassionately with Madanika. Unable to bear his lack of sexual interest, Kumbhaka said, "Every night I sleep next to you as a woman. I long to know pleasure known to a woman. So please make love to me as a husband makes love to a wife. This will not devalue your austerities because you have conquered desire." Shikhidhvaja consented to this, married Madanika, and made love to her. Every day, he would listen to wise words of Kumbhaka and every night he would make love to Madanika. One night, Kumbhaka decided to test the king's detachment. He used his magic powers to create an illusion of a bed on which lay Madanika making passionate love to a handsome stranger. The king saw them and turned away unmoved. "Sorry to disturb you. Please carry on," he said. Later, he told Madanika to find a man who could satisfy her passion. "I cannot, so let us remain friends as we were before." Delighted at the king's immunity to lust and anger, Madanika transformed into Cudala and revealed her identity and purpose. Shikhidhvaja was so impressed that he returned to his kingdom with his wife—who was both his teacher Kumbhaka and his lover Madanika—and ruled the land for ten thousand years with Cudala by his side.

Cudala is capable of taking both male and female forms but she finds that her husband relates to her intellectually only when she is male (Kumbhaka) and erotically only when she is female (Madanika).

Shikhidhvaja refuses to be his wife's student. He prefers knowledge coming from a man. Had he known right at the onset that Kumbhaka was his wife disguised he would not have been open to her teachings. Shikhidhvaja does not mind having sex with Madanika even though he is fully aware that Madanika is in essence male. The homosexual drift here is pretty obvious. Shikhidhvaja is reasonably groomed in the ascetic tradition not to initiate the affair. But he ends up making love to a man nevertheless, after he "becomes a woman" of course. When he discovers Madanika with another man, patriarchal values creep in. He rejects her. By then he is reasonably enlightened not to sour the rejection with bitterness or rage.

What emerges from the story of Chudala/Kumbhaka/Madanika is the role traditionally prescribed for men and for women. While men can be scholars and warriors—and by extension farmers, herdsmen, traders, and craftsmen—women can either be a whore or a wife, and are good only for sex, childbearing, and all things erotic. A woman joins Nature in creating new life. A man can father children, but he is also capable of something more. As a sage he can understand the workings of Nature, as a warrior he can lay claim over it, as a priest and sorcerer he can manipulate its forces, as a farmer and herdsmen he can domesticate its wildness and reap its bounty, and as an artisan and craftsman he can improvise on it. A woman is an extension of Nature. A man, though part of Nature, is also capable of breaking free from its inflexible rhythm. When Bhisma refuses to kill Shikhandi because he considers Shikhandi to be a woman, it is because killing woman is traditionally seen as an attack on Nature's procreative capacity. Bhisma—the man who had voluntarily turned away from his biological obligations—does not want to further antagonize Nature, and his forefathers, by destroying a female body that provides the dead a passage into the land of the living.

In the Hindu worldview, the capacity of man—and not woman—to dominate and break free from Nature is believed to stem from the difference in biology. Though, in general, Hindu philosophy considers the flesh to be merely clothes of the soul that are shed during death (reiterated in the popular pan-Hindu philosophical treatise *Bhagavad Gita*), the biology of the flesh plays a significant role in defining one"s spiritual and social status. The body, far from being a valueless shell of the soul, has for centuries been seen as a mystical vehicle that can be used for material growth and spiritual upliftment. It is the instrument of many occult practices. In the flesh lies the power that can make man *vira,* a heroic being who does not submit to Nature's impersonal rhythm.

Vira refers to both a material conqueror (a warrior, a farmer or herdsman, an artisan or craftsman) as well as a spiritual conqueror (an ascetic, a sorceror). Only a man can be a vira because he has access to semen (virya). Semen has magical properties. When spilt in a fertile womb it can create a child and when retained it can transform into a subtle substance known as *ojas* that rises up the spine, empowers the body, and illuminates the mind. The powerful body does not succumb to the limitations imposed by Nature. The enlightened mind is not fooled by illusory transformations of matter. Man thus has the capacity to manipulate the forces of the cosmos or break free from the cycle of rebirths. Women shed their seed every month, whether they want to or not. They lack the wherewithal to be viras. They are fettered to earth by menstrual blood forever. Hence, to confront Bhisma in battle, Amba needs male biology that can make her a warrior.

In most mystical and occult schools that rose in India, a woman was considered one step lower than a man in the evolutionary ladder. In Hinduism, Buddhism, and Jainism, the aspirant who seeks to break free from Nature and gain power over it, is invariably male. If Hindu goddesses such as Kali and Durga behave as warriors, bear weapons, and kill demons, it is only because goddesses are believed to be unaffected by the menstrual tide, hence possessing as much, if not greater, strength than the gods.

Hinduism, Buddhism, and Jainism rose from the same cultural matrix. Buddhism (path of the spiritually enlightened) and Jainism (path of the spiritual conqueror) are essentially monastic religions that seek to liberate all living creatures from the mundane world of rebirths. What is moksha (liberation from delusion) in Hinduism is, broadly speaking, what *nirvana* is to Buddhists and what *kaivalya* is to Jains. There are many deep differences between the three religions. Buddhism is agnostic, Jainism is atheistic, while Hinduism is theistic, atheistic, agnostic, and gnostic. While Buddha was the historical founder of Buddhism (500 B.C.E.), Jainism, as in Hinduism, has no fountainhead. The followers of the faith believe Jainism is an eternal truth (as Hinduism is to Hindus) that is revealed from time to time to wise men, purified over lifetimes. To attain the goal of liberation, Hinduism prescribes devotion, Buddhism prescribes meditation, and Jainism prescribes austerities, especially nonviolence.

Even though Hindus may insist that the soul is genderless and sex/gender is a material concept, material reality is invariably expressed through feminine symbols (the pot, the lotus, the conch, the sea, the serpent, the goddess), while spiritual reality is expressed through masculine symbols (the sun, the fiery pillar, the gods). Buddhists do not believe in the soul because it implies permanence. Nothing lasts forever in the Buddhist scheme of things. Not even gender, as the following story from Buddhist scripture *Vimalakirti* informs us. It concerns a great monk named Sariputra who is tested by a Buddhist goddess. It has been retold in Wendy Doniger's *Splitting the Difference*.

SARIPUTRA'S SEX CHANGE

A goddess turned Sariputra into a woman. He did not use his magic powers to revert back to his male form. The goddess then turned him back into a man and asked, "What happened to your female form?" and the wise Sariputra replied, "What happened to the male form earlier, happened to the female form later—it changed. I neither made it nor changed it."

Reality is thus viewed as a series of transformations. Nothing is static. Truth is illusory, as in "the pregnancy of a barren woman, the erection of eunuch, tracks of a flying bird." Even the Buddha said that in all things there is nothing male or female. Thus all identities, sex, and gender, are provisional. Despite such beliefs, Boddhisattvas become Boddhisattvas only after acquiring male bodies, and male minds. Biology matters.

All Jain Tirthankaras, spiritual conquerors who discover the "bridge of liberation," are male too. All except Malli-natha, say the scriptures. The following story of this female Tirthankara comes from *Jnatri-dharma-katha-sutra*, a Pali scripture dated. It has been retold by Padmanabh Jaini, in his book *The Jaina Path of Purification*.

MALLI WHO BECAME MALLI-NATHA

After completing worldly duties, King Mahabala and seven of his friends renounced the world and became Jain mendicants. They made a pact to take up an identical number of fasts as part of their austerities. However, because of ill health, Mahabala could not eat all his meals. He inadvertently fasted more than his friends and acquired more merit, enough to make him a Tirthankara in his next life. As these merits were acquired by breaking a pact, he was reborn with the body of a woman and named Malli, the jasmine-flower. Her beauty won her many suitors who went to war over her. Malli was so disgusted by the carnage resulting from lust for her body that she turned her back on worldly life and became a monk. Eventually she discovered the spiritual bridge that takes all creatures out of the material world. She crossed it and rose to the paradise of spiritual conquerors. Malli became Malli-natha.

Malli's exalted status is the reward for good karma (fasting), but his female body is the price of improper conduct (breaking a pact). In art, Malli-natha is usually depicted as male; the only sign of her femininity is her symbol, the jar. Only the more liberated Shwetambara sect of

Jains believe that Malli-natha was a woman. The austere Digambaras reject this idea. To them, all Tirthankaras are male. Only the male body has the wherewithal that enables the mind to liberate the soul from the shackles of karma.

Women can acquire male biology through *punya*. Male biology can be lost through paap. The word paap is commonly mistranslated as sin. There is no English synonym for punya. Punya is desirable and appropriate deeds that upholds social law and generates good karma. Paap is demeritorius conduct that results in the opposite. Just as good karma can transform man into a celestial being, it can also make a man out of a woman. Jain lore is full of tales where, depending on karma, rebirth is accompanied by change in sex. In the Jain *Ramayana,* the heroine Sita is reborn as a celestial man for enduring without complaint hardships that came in the wake of her wifely duties.[11] In the Jain *Mahabharata,* the man who breaks the nose of a Jain monk becomes Krishna's sister Ekanamsa in his next life, with a deformed nose that prevents her from getting married.[12]

But when Amba is reborn, she is not given a male body at birth. Why? Why, too, does the narrative incorporate an elaborate plot of sexual transformation? Scholars have observed that in Hindu lore and in Hindu law texts, rebirth may be associated with change in species, but rarely change in sex. Male humans are more likely to be reborn as male animals than as female humans. One of the few exceptions to this trend is the story where men who fell in love with the chaste Rama could make love to him only in their next birth when they were reborn as milkmaids and Rama had taken the form of Krishna (see Chapter 3).

Beliefs related to biology have generated social roles for men and women in the Hindu world. Male biology made priests, philosophers, protectors, and providers out of men. Female biology made women "mere" procreators. To become a warrior and avenge her fate, Amba needs to acquire a male body. To be taken seriously as a teacher, Chudala needs to transform into a man. The inability to dissociate social behavior from sexual biology lies at the heart of tales where women become men.

Chapter 2

Pregnant Kings

As Bhisma lay on a bed of arrows awaiting the hour of his death, the victorious Pandavas paid him a visit. Yudhishtira, the eldest Pandava, asked him questions on various worldly and otherworldly issues. The replies form the "Shanti Parva," an entire chapter of the *Mahabharata,* a compendium of ancient values and philosophies. One of the questions asked was, "Do men get more pleasure from sex or do women?" Bhisma replied that one had to rely on the testimony of Bhangashvana because only he had experienced pleasure both as a man and as a woman. The English translation of Bhangashvana's tale, which is quite similar to the Greek story of Teiresias, can be found in Johann Jakob Meyer's *Sexual Life in Ancient India.* A simpler retelling is found in Subash Mazumdar's *Who's Who in the Mahabharata.*

BHANGASHVANA: THE MAN WHO WAS FATHER AND MOTHER

King Bhangashvana performed a yagna so that he may be blessed with a hundred sons. The sacrifice pleased the celestial Devas and in due course, he fathered a hundred sons. Unfortunately, during the ceremony, he did not make an offering to Indra, king of the Devas. Furious, Indra cursed Bhangashvana and turned him into a woman. In due course, the female Bhangashvana bore a hundred sons. Thus, Bhangashvana ended up with two sets of children: those who called him "father" and those who called him "mother." When Indra found Bhangashvana happy in the company of two hundred children, he was further incensed. He hissed out a curse that the two sets of children would fight and kill each other. When this came to pass, Bhangashvana was inconsolable in grief. On learning of his lapse and the wrath of Indra, Bhangashvana made offerings of appeasement and begged that the children be revived. "I shall raise only one set of children. Which one shall it be: those who call you, 'father,' or those who call you, 'mother'?" asked the king of the Devas. "Let those who call me, 'mother' be revived," replied Bhangashvana. When asked why, Bhangashvana replied, "Because children love their mothers more than they love their fathers." Then Indra asked what would he like to be: a man or a woman. "A woman," he replied, explaining that women experience greater sexual pleasure than men during sex. Pleased with his honesty, Indra revived both sets of children.

Curses (and blessings) are common narrative tools used in Hindu lore to convey the idea of karma. They form the tangible link between actions and reactions. A blessing, earned by pleasing the gods, helps Bhangashvana father sons. A curse, resulting from overlooking Indra, turns him into a woman. But it is choice that keeps Bhangashvana a woman. Thus, the story of Bhangashvana is not just about sexual transformation; it is also about fate and free will.

Some say, in a Hindu world where everything is determined by past deeds, there is no such thing as free will. Others respond, while events are determined by past deeds, responses to events are products of free will. The latter approach forms the basis of a great many spiritual practices in India. We can choose to react positively, negatively, or not at all. Bhangashvana chooses to be a woman. He finds it a good thing. The reason given harks back to the time when women were believed to possess greater sexual desire than men and rules had to be created to control their voracious erotic appetite. The *Garuda Purana* (c. 900 C.E.) states an ancient misogynist adage, "women have twice the appetite of men, four times their cunning, and eight times their sexual craving." When Yudhishtira asks Bhisma about the sexual appetites of women, Bhisma narrates the testimony of the nymph Panchachuda who says that women, if unrestrained, will go to any man, even the old, infirm, and disabled. And if no man is available, they will fall on each other.[1]

In the following story, another man becomes a woman, this time through the power of piety. He also chooses to remain a woman but for another reason. The story comes from the *Skanda Purana* and is retold in Sadashiv Ambadas Dange's *Encyclopaedia of Puranic Beliefs and Practices,* Volume III, and in Vettam Mani's *Puranic Encyclopaedia.*

SOMAVAT: THE MALE WIFE

Sumedhas and Somavat were two poor Brahmins who sought wealth that would enable them to get a wife. They were directed to the generous queen Simantini who served lunch and offered rich gifts to one Brahmin couple daily. The two youths were in a fix—they needed the gifts to get married but they could not get the gifts from the queen unless they went to her with a bride. So they decided to obtain the gifts by deceit. Somavat disguised himself as a woman, and with Sumedhas acting as the husband, they introduced themselves to the queen as a "couple." Simantini, suspecting nothing, welcomed the two into the palace and treated them as a Brahmin couple, manifestations of Shiva and Shakti. Such was the power of the queen's piety that Somavat lost his manliness and became a woman. Sumedhas married his former friend. With the gifts they received, the two set up house and lived happily.

The cosmos transform the subterfuge into reality so as to uphold the dignity of Simantini's piety. Neither man protests against the sexual transformation. It is almost as if the transformation is mutually convenient. Somavat *wants* to be a woman. Sumedhas is glad he does. This seems odd when viewed in context of the general attitude toward women and womanhood in India throughout the ages. The greatest insult, even today, for a man is to be called a woman. Abuses such as, "Let him wear bangles," are hurled to prick male pride. When a man is referred to as a woman, it can mean that he is effeminate, impotent, incapable of performing with a woman, a non-man, a eunuch, a sexually dysfunctional male, a man who does not perform manly duties, or one who does not display manly qualities such as valor. Somavat's acceptance of his female body does suggest the fulfillment of a deep-seated desire to be Sumedhas' spouse.

In the *Rig Veda,* the oldest and most revered Hindu scripture, dated before the second millennium B.C.E., the male member is the subject of much praise. In it, a woman praises her husband's virile member (perhaps on restoration of his potency) in a brief, but vivid, verse: "His phallus appeared firm in front of him, that had been hanging down like a boneless thigh. Asanga's wife, Sasvati, seeing it, said, 'You have there, my lore, a splendid instrument of pleasure.' " [2] Latter-day commentaries inform us of the context of the praise.

According to Shaunaka's *Brhaddevata* (c. 400 B.C.E.), Asanga was a woman who had been turned into a man by a sage. Sayana, whose fourteenth-century commentary of the *Rig Veda* is much renowned, comes up with two stories. In the first story, Asanga is a prince who becomes a woman because of a curse and is transformed into a man because of a sage's grace. In the second story, Asanga's wife, unhappy with his impotency, performs austerities to make him potent. Both Shaunaka and Sayana seem to be equating impotency of a man with "emasculation" and "womanliness." By the grace of a sage, by the austerities of the wife, the "woman" becomes a "man," the impotent member becomes potent.

Praise is offered in the *Rig Veda* and in the *Brahmanas* (ritual texts based on Vedic verses) to the horse-headed Ashwin twins for imparting virility to husbands, for making men out of non-men, and for taking away their womanliness.[3] One cannot help but speculate, if these verses simply refer to men who are not sexually attracted to women. Are the prayers, incantations, rituals, and boons offering such men what modern-day Indian psychiatrists and sexologists promise homosexual men—the ability to father children?

India has a long tradition of associating the inability to father a child with lack of manliness or effeminacy, as the following story from the *Bhagavata Purana* (retold in Kamala Subramaniam's *Srimad Bhagavatam*) informs us.

SON OF A EUNUCH

During a gathering of the Yadavas in the city of Mathura, the clan priest Shyala was involved in a heated debate with sage Gargya. Before anyone could intervene, Gargya claimed he had been insulted by Shyala. When the Yadavas asked what exactly were the words spoken, Gargya replied, "He called me a eunuch." The Yadavas found this funny and laughed rather thoughtlessly. Piqued, Gargya left Mathura in a huff. He went to the forest and spent years consuming powdered iron to strengthen his semen. Then, by performing intense austerities, he invoked Shiva. "Let me father a son and prove Shyala wrong. And let this son of the so-called eunuch avenge his father's humiliation and destroy the city of the Yadavas." The god of destruction granted Gargya's wish. It so happened that King Yavanesha was childless. He invited Gargya to impregnate his wife. The child born of this union was dark as a beetle and named Kalayavana. Years later, he destroyed the city of Mathura, forcing the Yadavas to move to the island city of Dwaraka.

The word Yavana generally refers to the westerner and specifically to the Greeks who followed Alexander into India three hundred years before the common era. Yavanesha means "lord of the Greeks," while Kalayavana means the "black Greek," probably referring to a tribe of Indo-Greeks. The story clearly demonstrates how provocative the term "woman" or "non-man" is to a man. It strikes at the core of his masculinity. Hence, stories where men become women willingly or accept their female role without protest, suggest a deep-seated discomfort with the male sex or the masculine identity.

In the following story, a man becomes a woman because of an accident. The story is retold in Kamala Subramaniam's *Srimad Bhagavatam*, in Subash Mazumdar's *Who's Who in the Mahabharata*, and in Wendy Doniger's *Splitting the Difference*.

THE FOREST WHERE MEN BECAME WOMEN

Prince Sudyumna unwittingly entered a forest where Shiva and Parvati were making love. To prevent unwarrantable intrusions by sages that would embarrassed his consort, Shiva had cast a spell so that all those who entered the forest turned into women. When Sudyumna realized he had become a woman, he begged Shiva to reverse the spell. As spells cannot be reversed, only modified, Shiva decreed the female Sudyumna, or Ila, would alternate between man and woman for a month at a time, each time losing memory of the sexual transformation. Budha, lord of the planet mercury, son of the moon-god and the star-goddess, fell in love with Ila, the woman. When Ila turned into Sudyumna, the man, he wondered what he was doing in the forest. Budha lied that a storm had killed his servants and caused him to fall into a deep slumber. Such was Sudyumna's grief when he learnt about his servants that he decided to renounce the world and stay in the forest. So it came to pass: in the month Sudyumna turned into a woman, Budha made love to him/her and in the month he/she was a man, he/she spent time studying scriptures and practicing austerities under the guidance of Budha. In due course, Ila gave birth to Pururava whose sons went on to rule India. The descendants of Ila called themselves the Ailas.

The story of Sudyumna/Ila is a classic example of what scholars term "serial androgyny," transformation from one sex to another over time. The tale of Sudyumna/Ila is retold in the *Ramayana*, the *Mahabharata*, as well as in several *Puranas* (medieval chronicles of gods and kings dated from 500 to 1500 C.E.), indicating its importance. In every retelling, the story has undergone modification.

In the *Mahabharata*, Ila is the eldest daughter of Manu, the first king of the world, who became a man later in life, before turning into a woman in the enchanted forest. In the "Harivamsa" (a latter-day appendix of the *Mahabharata*), the daughter is born because the priest invoking the gods makes an error in the hymn; the error is later rectified and Sudyumna becomes male until he enters the enchanted forest. Thus Sudyumna/Ila's life is a case of female-to-male to female-to-male transformation. In the *Ramayana*, Ila is male right from the start, making the story a relatively straightforward case of male-to-female to male transformation.

In all these stories, Sudyumna/Ila does not want to be a woman. But he has to settle for a life of a serial androgyne with loss of memory of activities performed with his/her other biology. There is only one version—from the *Skanda Purana*—where Ila desires to be a woman and serve the goddess, but is made to change her mind by the goddess herself, who says that life as a woman was nothing but "curse and grief." Becoming or staying a man makes sense in a world where women are inferior.

There are remarkable similarities between this tale and the tale of Cudala/Kumbhaka/Madanika retold in Chapter 1. Sudyumna does what are traditionally considered to be manly things (study, self-develop), similar to Kumbhaka. But when he transforms into a woman, he does things that are considered womanly (have sex, produce children), similar to Madanika. As with Shikhidhvaja, Budha knows that his lover is in essence male, but that does not stop him from having sex with her. The sex stops as soon as the lover's male biology is restored. Appearances seem to matter more that the essence.

In the *Ramayana,* when Ila becomes male and loses memory of his female existence, Budha does not bother to inform him about the spell and the monthly transformations. Instead he lies, ensures Sudyumna stays in the forest, and makes love to him every time he turns into Ila. Could "Budha's lies" be an excuse for Ila's repression of his same-sex desires? Could this be a case of transexuality paving the way for realization of homosexual desires in heterosexual terms?

The *Bhagavata Purana* (c. 950 C.E.) informs us that eventually Sudyumna/Ila ascends to heaven, where he possess distinguishing signs of both men and women. In other scriptures, his/her eventual transformation to a male is stressed. It remains unclear whether the restoration of manhood is because he/she remembers the curse and propitiates Shiva, or because his/her kinsmen offer prayers and oblations to the gods.

The common element in all retellings is that the mother of the Ailas was also their father. In the *Mahabharata,* Ila has two sets of children—those fathered by his male form and those borne by his female form. The epic informs us that, at the insistence of sage Vasishtha, the children born of the female form succeed Sudyumna to the throne. This has led to euhemeristic explanations for Ila's androgyny, that Ila was Manu's daughter. Since latter-day patriarchy did not look favorably on a female founder, there was need to make the female ancestor male, hence the elaborate myth.

According to traditional sources, two lines of kings ruled the ancient plains of India—the solar dynasty fathered by Ikshavaku and the lunar dynasty mothered by Ila. Both Ikshavaku and Ila were the children of Manu, the first man. There are interesting differences between the solar and lunar dynasty of kings. Heroes such as Rama, who uphold social law at the cost of personal happiness, come from the solar line, whereas heroes such as Krishna, who play by their own rules, populate the lunar line. In legends of solar kings, the line between right and wrong is clearly defined. The line is blurred in cases of the lunar kings. With this in mind, it seems almost appropriate that the founder of the lunar line vacillate in the queer realm between masculinity and femininity.

The *Ramayana* reached its final form between 200 B.C.E. and 200 C.E. Though shorter than the *Mahabharata,* the *Ramayana* is more sophisticated in language and content. While the *Mahabharata* and its appendix, the "Harivamsa," revolve around the lives of lunar

kings, the *Ramayana* focuses on the tale of the greatest king of the solar dynasty—Rama. Similar to Krishna, Rama, is divinity incarnate, a
manifestation of the Vishnu on earth. Rama's August presence, however, contrasts the winsome wiliness of Krishna. The differences in
personality and approach to life, despite a common essence (Vishnu),
is attributed to the different ages they lived in. Rama walked the earth
at an earlier time, when dharma was more respected and the world
was less corrupt.

The *Ramayana* tells the story of Rama, the prince of Ayodhya who
abandons his claim to the throne and goes to the forest in deference to
the promise made by his father to his ambitious junior wife, Kaikeyi,
Rama's step-mother (a situation not unlike Bhisma's). Rama's dutiful
wife Sita and his brother Laxman follow him into the forest, where
for fourteen years they stoically contend with the wilderness. In the
final year of exile, the *Rakshasa*-king Ravana abducts Sita. The epic
then informs us how Rama and Laxman raise an army of monkeys,
cross the sea to the island of Lanka, make war with the Rakshasa, kill
Ravana, and rescue Sita.

To many, the story of Rama's exile is the story of the Aryanisation
of southern India since Rama's exile takes him from his kingdom in
the north over the Vindhya hills, across the Dandaka forest and the
Deccan plateau, beyond the Indian ocean to the island kingdom of
Lanka (traditionally believed but not archeologically proven to be the
island of Sri Lanka). An *Arya,* in Hindus scriptures, is a noble being
who respected the Vedic order of society and upheld dharma. Dharma
is sacred law based on the doctrine of duty and restraint. Rama is its
supreme upholder, rectitude personified, *maryada purushottam.* He
is chaste, obedient, noble, compassionate, and quite unlike his adver-
sary, the arrogant, brazen, fierce, and wild Ravana, the Rakshasa-
king, who follows the jungle law that "might is right," terrorizes
sages, kills kings, and rapes women, only to meet his match in the
more civilized Rama.

The monkeys who help Rama rescue Sita are led by Sugriva.
Sugriva and his elder brother Vali have a father not unlike Bhangashvana
and Sudyumna, a man who is also their mother. Before proceeding
further, we must understand what "monkey" means. The word for
monkey, *Vanara,* may have been derived from two words: forest
(vana) and man *(nara)*. It is suggested that the author of the epic took
a rather condescending artistic license to describe non-Aryan, but

helpful, southern tribes as "monkeys" to differentiate them from non-Aryan hostile tribes who were described as "demons" or Rakshasas. Jain Ramayanas find identification of Rakshasas with demons and Vanaras with monkeys rather fanciful, and they suggest that the monkeys were more likely to be distant relatives of the Rakshasas who distinguished themselves by carrying a monkey emblem on their banners.[4] The following story from Vettam Mani's *Puranic Encyclopaedia*, tells the story of how Sugriva and Vali were conceived by the union of two men.

THE DAWN-GOD BECOMES A WOMAN

Aruna, the dawn-god, charioteer of the Surya, the sun-god, heard that nymphs in the celestial city of Amravati planned to dance naked before Indra. As no man but Indra was allowed to watch the performance, Aruna gained entrance by taking the form of a woman called Aruni. When Indra saw Aruni he was so aroused that he made love to her and together they created a child called Vali. The next day, Aruna reported late for duty and Surya demanded an explanation. On learning of Aruna's transformation, Surya expressed his desire to see him as a woman. Aruna obeyed and Surya, too, fell in love with Aruni. They made love and created a child named Sugriva. Both children were given to Ahalya, wife of the sage Gautama. Gautama did not like them and turned them into monkeys who were then adopted by the monkey-king Riksharaja, ruler of Kishikinda.

The sexual transformation creates a situation for the conception of Vali and Sugriva through cross-sex intercourse. The gods do not seem to mind that the woman who arouses their lust is in essence male. This is reaffirmed in the following version of the tale retold by Wendy Doniger in her book *Splitting the Difference*. It comes from another retelling of the *Ramayana*.

RIKSHARAJA'S DIP INTO WOMANHOOD

One night, the monkey-king Riksharaja saw his reflection in a pond. Mistaking it for an enemy mocking him, he plunged into the water. When he came out, he was a beautiful woman. Indra, the rain-god, and Surya, the sun-god, saw her and were so over-

powered with lust that they shed their seed before they could
unite with her. The divine seeds transformed into children, nevertheless. Indra's seed fell on her hair *(vala)* and so the son born
of it came to be known as Vali. Surya's seed fell on her neck
(griva) and so the son born of it came to be known as Sugriva.
Later, Riksharaja reverted back to his original form. He suckled
the two children with honey and took them home. Thus Riksharaja
was both father and mother of his children.

In this tale, both species (monkey) and gender (male) change. The
children born, however, are simian.

It must be kept in mind that there are several versions of the
Ramayana; several hundred in fact. Even the "original" Sanskrit
work by the sage Valmiki is believed by most scholars to be only a retelling.[5] In each narration, the story is adapted to suit different sociocultural requirements. For example, in Valmiki's *Ramayana*, it is said
that after Sita is rescued from the clutches of Ravana, Rama abandons
her because his subjects feel her reputation has been compromised by
her long sojourn with another man. This controversial conclusion of
the epic is rarely retold in modern retellings of the epic, as in Kamala
Subramaniam's *Ramayana*. When told, as in Ramanand Sagar's television serial *Uttar Ramayana,* every effort is made to delink this episode
from the main plot, the triumph of Rama over Ravana. In one Southeast
Asian version of the epic, the *Ramakirti,* Vali and Sugriva are conceived
because the sage Gautama's wife Ahalya has adulterous liaisons with
Indra and Surya. When Gautama discovers the cuckoldry, he curses
the two children to become monkeys. Thus, sexual transformation is
not a necessary motif in all retellings of the birth of Vali and Sugriva.
What purpose, then, does the sexual transformation of Riksharaja and
Aruni in other retellings serve?

In all three versions of the birth of Vali and Sugriva, Indra fathers
the former and Surya the latter. Thus, the divine origin of the monkey-kings who aid Rama is established. The mother, in the first two
cases, is not quite a woman but rather a biologically transformed man
whose beauty enchants the gods. In the third version, the mother is an
oversexed woman, an adulteress. The monkey-kings are both divine
and imperfect (androgyne/adulteress). Their simian nature is explained
by a curse, or by the fact that their father was a monkey. Why this
need to add elements of divinity, imperfection, bad karma, and even
bestiality in the origins of the monkey-kings? Perhaps, their "queer"

and cursed origins established their "barbarian" status. Their "divine" origins differentiated them from the much hated Rakshasas, explained their benevolence toward the hero Rama, and made them acceptable to the Vedic audience.

Both Vanars and Rakshasas are animal-like (and hence barbarians) because they follow the *matsya nyaya* (the law of the wild, where big fish eat small fish). Their leaders assume power by killing or driving away rivals. Ravana drives his brother Kubera away to be lord of Lanka, while Vali drives Sugriva away to become king of Kishkinda. Their sexual and violent instincts are unrestrained by any sense of law or duty. They do not respect marital fidelity (Ravana abducts Sita, Vali makes Sugriva's wife Ruma his own). Rama, on the other hand, though part of the material world, bridles himself with the principles of dharma and does not succumb to the throbbing sensuousness of samsara.

In the following story based on the *Puranas,* a man is transformed into a woman so that he learns what it means to be swept away by the force of samsara. There are many variations of this story, and Narada does not become a woman in all of them. Sometimes he just succumbs to the charm of a woman, becomes a householder, gets embroiled in worldly matters, and forgets the divine.

NARADA BECOMES A WOMAN

Narada once asked Vishnu, "What is this thing they call maya?" In response, Vishnu asked Narada to fetch him some water from a river to quench his thirst. While collecting the water, Narada slipped and fell into the river. When he came out, he had acquired the body of a woman. A man looked at him admiringly and Narada became aware of his feminine charm. The stranger begged Narada to marry him. Narada accepted the proposal, became a wife, and gave birth to many children. Together, they built a house and established a prosperous farm on the riverbank. Surrounded by a loving husband, happy children, and a prosperous household, Narada experienced great joy. Then one day, after torrential rains, the river broke its banks and washed the farm away. Narada's husband and children were drowned in the flood. When the waters receded, Narada collected the corpses of her loved ones and carried them to a riverside crematorium. As she was about to the light the funeral pyre, she experienced an extraordinary hunger. She looked around for some food and found a mango on the highest branch of a tree. To get to it, she piled the bodies of her husband and children on top of each other and climbed the pyramid of corpses. As she reached for the fruit, she slipped and fell into the river. "Help me, help me," she cried. Instantly, Vishnu pulled Narada out of the water. Narada suddenly found himself in Vishnu's presence with his male body restored. "Where is the water I sent you for?" asked Vishnu. Narada looked at the empty pot in his hand and realized how attachment to his female form and the sensual pleasures he had derived from it had caused him to forget all about his mission. Vishnu smiled, for Narada had understood the meaning and power of maya.

Maya is delusion—the false interpretation of sensory stimuli by a mind governed by the ego. To realize the truth, the ego has to be conquered and the mind controlled. In Hinduism, as in Jainism and Buddhism, the mind is given great importance. The mind can ascertain outer material reality; it can also perceive inner spiritual reality. Mind is the one thing over which man can control. It helps man make choices. Thus, through mental control one can repress desires, fulfill duties, and uphold dharma. Furthermore, through manipulation of mental activities (also known as yoga), man can gain control over the material world or break free from it by realizing the spiritual world.[6]

Material reality or Nature, referred to as samsara or *prakriti,* is the world of sex and violence, name and form, governed by space and time, where everything transforms, is born, and eventually dies. Spiritual reality, known as the *brahman* (in *Upanishads*) or *purusha* (in yoga), is everything matter is not. It is the principle that is unaffected by space or time; it has no attributes, cannot be contained within a definition, and is essentially pure consciousness, absolute knowledge, eternal stillness, unending serenity, and unconditional bliss.[7] The tumultuous power of the material world is roused or restrained through fertility rites based on symbolic sex (floral offerings) and ritual violence (blood sacrifice), the aim being to acquire pleasure, prosperity, and power. The still wisdom of the spirit is realized through continence, nonviolence, restraint, devotion, meditation, and monastic principles.

Though theoretically aniconic and beyond attribute *(nirguna),* in the mythological realm, spirit acquires form, becomes godhead contained within (male) biology, and defined by a (male) gender. The rest becomes female and feminine.

Traditionally, samsara is depicted by feminine characters (nymphs, goddesses) and symbols that suggest motion (e.g.,water, lotus, conch, pots, circles, spirals, dots, red color, and downward pointing triangles). Spiritual reality has been depicted by masculine characters (sages, gods) and symbols that suggest stability (e.g., staff, fire, pillars, squares, upward pointing triangles, white color, and instruments that cut and pierce).

Narada is no ordinary sage; he is the mind-born son of the creator Brahma.[8] This means no woman has participated in his birth. The female seed has not contributed to his biology. He is an immaculate conception and was never nurtured in a womb. Narada is as *ayonija*, one-not-born-of-the-womb. Since the womb is the gateway into the cycle of rebirths, Narada is untouched by space and time, unfettered by samsara, and unaffected by the fear of death. He retains his purity and the resulting wisdom by resolutely staying away from the householder's life, preferring the ascetic path instead. In Hindu lore, Narada plays a rather "puckish" role. He is a meddlesome sage and a busybody who creates trouble wherever he goes. He is an agent of karma—he makes events happen. His gossip stirs events and helps rotate the wheel of existence. Narada ensures his detachment through devotion or *bhakti;* he knows that the only truth is Vishnu and all else is maya.

By describing Narada, and other mind-born children of Brahma, as males, ancient narrators have implicitly suggested that the more masculine one is the more liberated one is from samsara and that the more feminine one is the more fettered one is to the wheel of existence. This is made explicit in the story of Narada. When Narada falls into water, the ancient (feminine) symbol of the demiurge, his celestial male body is replaced by an earth-bound female body. This body is flooded with sensations and emotions that make him forget Vishnu and trap him in samsara.

The concept of ayonija plays a crucial role in Hindu lore. The non-womb born is a special creature, usually male, who is not subject to the transformations of samsara. Unlike womb-born mortals, death does not affect him, change does not frighten him. He possesses enough spiritual wisdom and serenity to not be overwhelmed by material events.

There are different types of ayonijas in Hindu lore, some more earthbound than others. Foremost among them are the *sapta rishis,* seven seers of universal knowledge, who are Brahma's mind-born sons. These seers, it is believed, transmitted universal cosmic knowledge *(sanatan dharma)* in the form of a collection of hymns (the *Vedas*) that help mortals cope with the terrors of material reality: death and change. It is believed that the rishis, inspired by spiritual reality, came up with ideas such as dharma (social law) and yoga (mystical techniques) that helps in either containing the wildness of samsara or transcending it.

Sages such as Agastya and Drona are also ayonija. They are conceived when their fathers—usually gods or seers—shed semen (usually in a pot, symbol of the womb) upon sighting naked nymphs.[9] The seed in these cases is potent enough through continence and austerity to transform into a male child. Women neither nurture nor nurse them into life. They, too, are immaculate, but are more earthbound than surs because women inspire their birth. The Devas are even more earthbound because they have a mother—Aditi, the wife of the primal mage Kashyapa (see Chapter 3). The gods bypass the womb and leave their mother's body from her side in order to acquire the status of ayonija, albeit of a slightly lower variety. Great kings could also be ayonija, as the following story of Yuvanashva from the *Mahabharata* informs us. The English translation of the tale can be found in Johann Jakob Meyer's *Sexual Life in Ancient India.* A simpler retelling is found in Subash Mazumdar's *Who's Who in the Mahabharata.*

YUVANASHVA: THE PREGNANT KING

King Yuvanashva had several wives, but no children. Feeling sorry for him, sages prepared a pitcher of magic water that had the power to makes his wives pregnant. When the king visited the sages, he was so overcome by thirst that he accidentally drank the magic water and became pregnant. Nine months later, he experienced labor pain. There was no orifice through which the child could emerge. Yuvanashva invoked Ashwini, the divine physician, who cut his side open and pulled out the baby. "How do I nurse him?" Yuvanashva asked. In response, Indra, king of the Devas, cut his finger. Out flowed milk. Indra let the newborn suckle his finger. The child born of a man, delivered by gods, and nursed by another god grew up to be Mandhatri, the great one.

No woman participates in Mandhatri's birth or arouses his father. No female seed contributes to his biology and he is not nurtured in a womb. Even the midwife and nursemaid are not female. The story of Yuvanashva's unilateral pregnancy implies that Mandhatri owed his greatness to his lack of contamination by anything female.

Mandhatri is described as an ancient king of the solar line—an ancestor of Rama—revered for upholding dharma in his kingdom. In traditional reconstructions of Indian history, such as N.S. Rajaraman's new chronology of ancient India (based on data from the *Ramayana, Mahabharata,* and the *Puranas*), it is said that Mandhatri ruled India even before Rama and Krishna. His golden age is dated around the fifth millennium B.C.E. This reconstruction rejects the idea proposed by European Orientalists (based on comparative philology applied to Vedic scriptures) that Aryans invaded India and established the Vedic civilization around 2000 B.C.E., by displacing an indigenous Dravidian culture.[10]

Another great king who was born without the intervention of women was Prithu. The *Bhagavata Purana* states that Prithu was churned out of the body of a dead king by the seven cosmic seers. The king, Vena, was a corrupt being who did not uphold dharma. The sages rose in revolt and had him killed. They then churned his corpse, strained out all the corruption, and from the remainder pulled out a man who was consecrated as king of the earth. Prithu is also born without the association of anything female. Being ayonija, it is easier for him to bridle his senses, restrain his ego, and uphold dharma. Unlike his father, he is not susceptible to the charms of Nature. Desire cannot overpower his sense of duty. The gods therefore bestow upon him a bow, a symbol of authority over earth. When the earth refuses to let seeds germinate and plants fructify, Prithu raises his bow, threatens the earth with his arrow, domesticates her, promises to respect her bounty by instituting dharma, and forces her to yield her wealth. Not surprisingly, Prithu is considered a manifestation of godhead.[11]

Female ayonijas are not as common as male ayonijas; they are usually goddesses who manifest on earth. A case in point is Sita, the wife of Rama, an incarnation of the goddess Laxmi, Vishnu's consort. In the *Valmiki Ramayana,* it is said she was found in a furrow when her father Janaka was ritually plowing the sacred fields of the mother-goddess (in Sanskrit, sita = furrow).[12] The following story of her birth comes from a Kannada retelling of the *Ramayana*. It has been retold in A. K. Ramanujan's essay "Three Hundred Ramayanas," compiled by Vinay Dharwadker.

RAVANA'S PREGNANCY

> Ravana was childless. So he approached a sage who gave him a magic mango that would make his wife pregnant. On the way to Lanka, Ravana experienced such great hunger that he ate the mango himself and became pregnant. His pregnancy advanced a month each day. On the ninth day he sneezed and out came a baby girl. The oracles said that the girl would be the cause of death, so Ravana put the girl in a box and buried her in a field. Janaka plowed her out and adopted this girl.

The traditional bards who narrate this tale say that Sita was called Sita because she was born when her father sneezed (in Kannada, sita = sneeze). This tale adds an incestuous dimension to Ramayana. Sita's abductor is actually her father. This twist is used to explain why Sita was never physically molested by Ravana. It must be kept in mind that even the suggestion that the modesty of Sita, who has been elevated to the status of a goddess, was outraged during her sojourn in Lanka is unacceptable to the devout Hindu. The story is that Ravana's father recognized his daughter by a birthmark's, but was too proud to submit before Rama.

Getting back to the male ayonija. Purification from all things feminine, hence worldly, helped one acquire spiritual knowledge that enabled one to manipulate or transcend the material world. This belief gave rise to initiation ceremonies where the aspirant underwent a ritual death (of the biological body delivered by a woman, his mother) and a ritual rebirth (from the spiritual body of a man, his teacher). This was the *upanayana* ceremony, a rite of passage when a man became *dvija* or "twice born," this time delivered through the Vedic knowledge given by the teacher.[13] In the *Atharva Veda*, dated around 1000 B.C.E., we find the lyrics: "The teacher, taking him (the student) in charge, makes the Vedic student an embryo within; he bears him in his belly three nights; the gods gather unto him to see him when born."

The idea of a teacher giving birth to a student is explicit in the following story of Shukra, the guru of the demons, who acquired the hymn to conquer death, the mrityunjaya, from Shiva, the god of destruction himself. This story is found in the *Mahabharata* and the *Vamana Purana* (c. 450-900 C.E.). It has been retold in Stella Kramrisch's *The Presence of Shiva*.

SHIVA GIVES BIRTH TO SHUKRA

> Kavya sought the hymn that revives the dead, so he propitiated Shiva, hanging himself head down over a smoky fire. When Shiva arrived, Kavya slipped into Shiva's mouth. For eons he remained in Shiva's belly. Shiva performed austerities and the power of the austerity permeated into Kavya's being. At long last, having discovered the secret hymn, Kavya sought a way to get out. The passage open was the penis. As Kavya emerged, Shiva caught him and decided to kill him. Shiva was stopped by his consort, Parvati, who said, "As he has left your body through your penis, he is your son." Thus Kavya came to be known as Shukra, the male seed.

Kavya gains knowledge only when he becomes an embryo in his teacher's body. In the teacher's womb, he is nurtured into wisdom and given a new life. Biological birth through the body of a mother gives man one view of life, one that frightens and makes him insecure. Intellectual rebirth through the body of a teacher gives him another view of life, one that enables him to conquer his fears and insecurities. Rebirth through a man's mind is thus seen as superior to birth through a woman's body.

Kavya, or Shukra, is the lord of the planet Venus. While in other cultures Venus is female, Shukra is male. But he remains the source of all things traditionally associated with femininity: intuition, creativity, eroticism. He has only one eye, suggestive of a lack of rationality. He serves as preceptor of Asuras, the earthbound or chthonian beings. His rival sage Brihaspati—lord of the planet Jupiter, hence rationality—serve Devas, celestial beings who are eternal enemies of the Asuras (Chapter 3). Shukra was not only born of a man, he gave birth to a man too, as the following story from the *Mahabharata* and retold in Subhash Anand's "Story as Theology" informs us. It is the story of how the wily Devas tricked the guru of the Asuras into giving away the hymn of rejuvenation.

KAVYA GIVES BIRTH TO KACHA

Empowered by the hymn of rejuvenation, Kavya brought back
to life all the Asuras who fell in battle against the Devas. Distraught at the state of affairs, the king of the Devas, Indra, ordered his son Kacha to learn the magic formula by fair means or
foul. Kacha presented himself in the hermitage of Kavya disguised as a Brahmin and enrolled himself as a student. Kacha's
obedience, dedication, and devotion impressed Kavya, but not
enough to part with the hymn. Meanwhile, Kavya's daughter,
Devayani, fell in love with Kacha while the Asuras discovered
his true identity. The Asuras ambushed and killed Kacha. Unable to bear his daughter's grief, Kavya brought Kacha back to
life. Determined to get rid of Kacha, the Asuras killed him once
again. This time they cut his body and tricked Kavya into eating
him. When Devayani realized what had been done, she begged
her father to restore Kacha once again. "He now resides within
my body. If I revive him, he will emerge by killing me. The only
solution is that you teach him the magic formula as soon as he
emerges so that he can bring me back to life." Devayani did as
she was told. First, Kavya used the hymn to revive Kacha, dying
in the process. Then Kacha, after learning the hymn from
Devayani, restored Kavya. Devayani was so happy that she
begged Kacha to accept her as his wife. "I would love to, but
now that Kavya has given birth to me I am his son and that
makes me your brother. Marriage between brother and sister is
not right." Kacha then went back to his father. The Devas now
were equally matched against the Asuras.

In their quest to kill the son of Indra, the Asuras inadvertently facilitate his rebirth through the body of their guru. Devayani's love for
Kacha ensures his resurrection, but in what ensues *her* father ends up
becoming *his* mother, making it impossible for her love to be realized. What takes Kacha away from Devayani is what gives Kacha
power over death. Thus, male pregnancy (purification from all things
material) results in separation from a woman (symbol of material existence) and gives power over death (curse of material existence).

Material reality in Hinduism is the medium through which spiritual reality expresses itself. Material reality is also the means through
which spiritual reality can be realized. Depending on the path taken,
Hinduism can be broadly divided into two schools of thought: the Ve-

dic or the Tantrik. Both view material reality as feminine. In the Vedic path, material reality is a nymph who distracts the aspirant with her solicitations. In the Tantrik path, material reality is a teacher who enlightens the aspirant through her charms. In both schools, the aspirant is male and the female facilitates spiritual growth as enchantress or as instructor. Devayani, as with material reality, helps and enchants Kacha; she gives him life, she offers him love. In doing so she gives him power over death, but ends up losing him. The story captures the ambiguous attitude of Hinduism toward woman and material reality. Both are necessary for existence. Both make life wonderful. Ultimately, however, both need to be overpowered and transcended.

The upanayana ceremony transformed a boy into a brahmachari, the seeker of truth. Guided by his teacher—his spiritual father and mother—he discovered answers to life's mysteries in Vedic scriptures. During this period, to make himself worthy of the divine knowledge, the student was expected to avoid contamination from everything that could fetter him (really or symbolically) to the material world. Since sex and violence govern the transformations of Nature, brahmacharya involved staying away from all things remotely sexual (e.g., women, intercourse, flowers, spices, wine) or violent (e.g., blood, death, war, anger).

The greatest brahmachari in the Hindu pantheon is the ascetic-god Shiva, lord of destruction. He destroys everything that makes one earthbound. He even beheaded Brahma for creating the first woman, Shatarupa, desiring her and placing his seed in her womb. Artists have visualized him as an ash-smeared hermit who rides a bull, meditates atop an icy peak wrapped in animal skins, and dances with goblins in the light of funeral pyres. His stern visage, the trident in his hand, the snake round his neck, his rattle-drum, and his fondness for hemp and poison flowers frighten away women who desire him. He is hardly husband or lover material. On his forehead is a third eye—perfectly symmetrical—symbolizing his power of discrimination and transcendence. The two eyes that are seduced by the material world are shut. The third eye that perceives spiritual reality is open. Untouched by samsara, unaffected by prakriti, his seed has remained unspilt for eons. Transforming into the nectar of wisdom, it has moved up his spine and helped the lotus of consciousness bloom in his head. The drawn-up semen, the roused yet retained seed, is indicated in art by an erect phallus. The resulting virile energy manifests as thick matted hair that adorns Shiva's head. When the moon-god's luster started to wane after being cursed by his father-in-law with impotency for favoring only one of his wives, the moon-god sought refuge in Shiva's locks, regained his virility, and began to wax. Hence, in images, the crescent moon always rests on Shiva's head. Shiva is, in Hindu lore, the personification of manhood because he has not succumbed to the charms of womanhood.

Yet, Shiva is also a householder. He has a wife. Two of them in fact: the mountain princess Parvati/Gauri who sits on his left lap and the river-nymph Ganga who lies trapped in his matted locks. He also has two sons: the warrior-god Karitkeya and the elephant-headed Ganesha. To understand this enigma of the erotic ascetic, to fathom this hermit-householder, we must now turn to Subrahmaniam, the greatest ayonija vira.

In the *Mahabharata*, when Amba set about looking for a champion who would defeat Bhisma, she invoked Subrahmaniam, the lance-bearing divine warlord who leads the Devas in their battles against the Asuras. Subrahmaniam gave her a garland of lotuses and said, "He who wears this garland will be the cause of Bhisma's death." Amba took the garland from the court of one king to another. But despite the assured grace of Subrahmaniam no man dared face Bhisma. In disgust, Amba discarded the garland and deserted the world of man. She put the garland around her neck in her next life when she was born as Drupada's daughter/son Shikhandini/Shikhandi (see Chapter 1). The story of Subrahmaniam's garland is told in Subash Mazumdar's book, *Who's Who in the Mahabharata*, and Kamala Subramaniam's *Mahabharata*.

Subrahmaniam was the divine patron of warriors in ancient India. As with the Greek Ares, he is associated with war, virility, and the planet Mars. His symbols—a lance, a jungle fowl, and a peacock—radiate male power. Also known as Kartikeya (ward of the Krittika nymphs), Kumara (the adolescent), Guha (mysterious one), Skanda (jet of semen), and Sanmukha (six-headed one), he is a virile god, renowned for his good looks, his valor in battle, and his esoteric wisdom. In his oft-quoted book *Gods of Love and Ecstasy: The Traditions of Shiva and Dionysus*, Alain Danielou described him as a "god whose only wife was his army, whose cult was forbidden to women and who was a favorite deity of homosexuals."[14] This conclusion—though empowering to many in queer circles—is debatable since, in my opinion, Danielou has confused the

North Indian Kumaraswami/Kartikeya whose cult is forbidden to women with the South Indian (Tamil) Murugan/Subrahmaniam, who is widely worshipped by the Hijra-like Alis of Tamil Nadu. Though the two gods are theoretically identical, there are significant differences in their ritual manifestation in North and South India.

The story of Kartikeya/Subrahmaniam's birth has many versions. It has transformed over time. In the earliest version found in the *Mahabharata,* he is the son of the fire-god Agni, born through the fusion of six jets of semen spurted at the sight of six women, the chaste wives of the seven celestial seers. He is thus super-masculine, six men fused in one, born untouched by the female seed, and without the aid of a womb. In the *Puranas,* written when theism was becoming more popular than Vedic gods and rituals, Shiva superceded Agni in importance and appropriated his deeds. He became Kartikeya's father. The following story contains dominant motifs found in all the major retellings, including the most popular one found in *Shiva Purana.* Various versions of the birth of Kartikeya can be found in the book *Shiva: The Erotic Ascetic* by Wendy Doniger O'Flaherty.

BIRTH OF KARTIKEYA

An Asura named Taraka had obtained a boon that only a six-day-old boy could kill him. The boon made him near immortal. He attacked and defeated the Devas and drove them out of their celestial city Amravati. The Devas wondered where they could get a child who could fight a battle on the seventh day of his life. "Only Shiva can father such a child. His semen retained for eons and resplendent with the powers of his austerities can bring forth such a warrior." So they begged the mother-goddess to transform into Parvati, the mountain-princess, enchant Shiva out of his cave, marry him, and draw out his seed through lovemaking. After great difficulty the goddess managed to become the hermit-god's bride. As householder, Shiva made love to Parvati. Though they were united for hundreds of years, Shiva never shed his seed. Alarmed, the Devas sought the help of the fire-god Agni who went into Shiva's cave and interrupted his lovemaking in the form of a bird. Embarrassed by the intrusion, Parvati turned away from Shiva. At that moment, Shiva let loose a jet of semen that Agni caught in his mouth. When Parvati saw this she was furious. "Only I have the right to nurture this seed.

The Devas have deprived me of my child. So, let them never father children. Instead, let them know what it means to be pregnant." Shiva's seed that had entered Agni's body consequently seeped into the bodies of all the Devas and they become pregnant. The pain was unbearable so they begged for mercy. After much placation, Shiva's seed left the body of the Devas and re-entered Agni. At that moment, six of the seven wives of the seven cosmic seers were seated next to the holy fire to ward off the cold. Though the fire-god's heat and light, the seed of Shiva seeped into the bodies of these six women. When the seers discovered that their wives were pregnant, they accused the women of adultery and drove them away. In anger, each woman cast the fetus out of her body and into the river Ganges. Such was the fury of the cast-away fetus that the river water started to boil and the forest of reeds on its banks caught fire. Within the smoldering ash, the fetuses merged and transformed into a six-headed, twelve armed child. At first the six abandoned wives of the seers—known as Krittikas—tried to kill the child but when they saw him their breasts oozed milk. They ended up nursing him instead. Parvati, Agni, Ganga, and the Krittikas fought for custody of the child. Shiva said he belonged to all since all had helped in creating him. This mighty child born of Shiva's seed, became a man in six days. On the seventh day, he picked up a lance, challenged Taraka to battle, and killed him.

Shiva's celibacy makes his seed powerful. His lovemaking draws it out, but the Devas do not want the child to be touched by female seed or held in a womb. The stated reason is a fear that the cosmos will not have the power to sustain a child born of Shiva *and* Parvati. The implied reason is a fear of contamination, so they interrupt the lovemaking and walk away with the male seed. The goddess in her rage curses the gods to become pregnant and lose the ability to father children. The gods experience the pains of labor and beg for mercy. The fiery seed of Shiva burns even fire, makes six women pregnant, boils the icy Ganga, and sets the river of reeds on fire. So powerful is Shiva's seed that no container—neither fire nor water nor the six wombs of the Krittikas—is capable of holding it. So powerful is the seed that it transforms into a virile warrior on the seventh day of its life.

The story goes that after killing the demons, Kartikeya was so pampered by his mother Parvati that he became wayward and began casting his lustful attentions on the wives of the gods. This tale from the *Brahmanda Purana* (c. 350 to 900 C.E.) is retold in the *Puranic Encylopaedia* of Vettam Mani.

KARTIKEYA TURNS AWAY FROM WOMEN

> After the war, Kartikeya was so full of energy that, finding no outlet, he became lustful and sought the embrace of every woman he met. He did not even spare the wives of the gods. Unable to bear his unwarrantable attentions, the women complained to Parvati. To stop her son, she made sure that every time he tried to force himself on a woman he saw only the face of his mother. Kartikeya left the women alone.

This projection of motherhood on every woman prevents Kartikeya from looking upon any woman erotically. He loses interest in women and prefers the company of his army. In deference to his discomfort in the presence of women, only men are allowed to enter his shrine. Another reason why women do not worship Kartikeya is that he is associated with war that makes widows of women. Further, in Hindu astrology, *Jyotisha shastra,* women whose horoscope is governed by Mars or Mangal, the planet of Kartikeya, are believed to end up as widows early in life. Turning away from women and preferring the company of soldiers has given Kartikeya a homoerotic aura in many queer circles.

The practice of preventing women from entering Kartikeya's shrine is prevalent mainly in North India, where the worship of the divine warlord is on the wane. In South India, especially in the state of Tamil Nadu, where the cult of the youthful warlord is extremely popular, Kartikeya or Subrahmaniam has two wives: Valli and Devasena.

According to one tradition, Kartikeya was furious when his father let his younger brother, Ganapati, marry before him. He left Shiva's abode in the Himalayan range and went south. In the North Indian tradition, he settled on the southern Krauncha mountain, refusing to speak to his parents. In the South Indian tradition, he moved further south where he eventually married two women and settled down. Kartikeya's first wife, Devasena, was the daughter of Indra, king of the gods. She was given in marriage to Subrahmaniam as a reward for his valor in battle. His second wife, Valli, was a local girl, a tribal maiden. The tale of her courtship by Kartikeya is extremely popular in Tamil Nadu. The word Devasena means "army of the gods," while the name Valli is believed to be derived from the word "vel" or lance, in Tamil. The wives of the divine warlord may be seen as personifications of his army and his weapons. They may be viewed as shakti, emanations of personal power embodied in female form, and not true wives.

The marriage to Devasena links the warrior-god with the celestial regions, and the marriage to Valli binds Subrahmaniam to earthly realms. Standing between the two women, he becomes the lord of heaven and earth. Tamils worship him in the form of a cherubic boy with curly hair holding a spear, or as a virile man flanked by two wives. Kartikeya is also adored as the supreme keeper of mystical wisdom because he knew the meaning of a sacred chant that was not known even to his father. The Alis of Tamil Nadu follow the local tradition and adore Murugan. Confusion between the North Indian Kartikeya, who distanced himself from women, and the South Indian Murugan, who was extremely popular among Tamilian Alis, may have led Alan Danielou to conclude that Kartikeya/Subrahmaniam was a popular god among homosexuals.

The idea of unilateral male pregnancy with (Bhagashvana) or without (Yuvanashva) the acquisition of female biology may be seen as a narrative expression of womb-envy or of a desire to be independent of women. But such a psychoanalytic interpretation diverts attention from the symbolic value given to maleness and femaleness in Hindu art, ritual, and lore. Throughout the ages, the male form has been identified with the spiritual principle and the female form with the material world. From a spiritual point of view, everything material, hence feminine, came to be seen as contamination. In the pregnant male, desirable qualities of the spirit (wisdom, serenity, permanence) merge with desirable qualities of matter (creation). The queer sexuality in tales of men who become women and men who become pregnant thus communicates a primal need to sublimate the humiliating passivity man is subjected to when confronted with the impersonal and awesome transformations of Nature.

Women in Amorous Embrace. Temple carving, Khajuraho, Madhya Pradesh.
Courtesy of the Archeological Survey of India. Author's collection.

Agni Drinking Shiva's Semen. Temple carving, Orissa, twentieth century. Courtesy of Orissa State Museum, Bhubaneshwar.

Kartikeya. Calendar art, twentieth century. Author's collection.

Subramanium with Vali and Sena. Calendar art, twentieth century. Author's collection.

Vishnu As the Enchantress Mohini. Temple wall carving, Hoyasaleshwara temple, Halebid, Karnataka.

Ayyappa. Calendar art, twentieth century. Author's collection.

Krishna Being Cross-Dressed by His Companions, the Milkmaids. Calendar reprint of an eighteenth-century Kanga painting. Author's collection.

Sakhibhava, a Man Dressed As a Milkmaid in His Desire to Realize Krishna, the Divine Cowherd. Photo © Dolf Hartsuiker, from his book *Sadhus: India's Holy Men,* published by Inner Traditions International, Rochester, Vermont, and by Thames and Hudson, Ltd., London, 1993.

Bahucharaji-Mata Riding a Rooster. Calendar art, twentieth century. Author's collection.

A Sage with a Naked Man (Whom He Threatens to Castrate?). Temple carving, Khajuraho, Madhya Pradesh. Courtesy of the Archeological Survey of India. Photographed by Aniruddha Kudalkar.

Jogappa, a Male-to-Female Cross-Dresser Who Serves the Goddess Yellamma.
Photographed by Barbara Lloyd, from *Colours of Southern India*, published by
Thames and Hudson, London, September 1999.

Ardhanareshwara, with the Female Half on the Left Side and the Male Half on the Right Side. Folk art, Orissa, twentieth century. Author's collection

Shiva's Earrings, Left Side Female. Chola bronze, twentieth century. Author's collection.

Chapter 3

Cross-Dressing Tricksters

On the fifth day of the annual Brahmotsavam celebrations at Tirumala in the southern state of Andhra Pradesh (India's richest temple), the presiding deity, Vishnu (locally known as Venkateshwara Balaji), is taken out in a grand procession bedecked as the celestial enchantress Mohini.[1] In another town to the north of India, Nathdvara, in the desert state of Rajasthan, in the temple of Shrinathji, the presiding deity, Krishna, is draped in female apparel *(sakhi-vesha)* in a secret ceremony, away from prying eyes.[2] To place the ritual cross-dressing of the two deities in context, it is essential to understand what role Vishnu and Krishna play in the Hindu pantheon. This cannot be done without clarifying the concept of god, goddess, and godhead in Hinduism.

Vishnu is not an ordinary god, or Deva, such as the rain-god Indra or the fire-god Agni we have encountered in earlier chapters. He is godhead personified, Bhagavan. To some, Bhagavan is without form and to others, godhead has form—both male and female. The male form embodies the transcendental otherworldly aspect of the divine (the cause), while the female form embodies the tangible earthbound aspect of the divine (the manifestation). The male aspect of godhead is instrumental; it creates (Brahma), sustains (Vishnu), and destroys (Shiva) the world thus setting the wheel of existence (samsara) in motion. The female aspect of godhead (Devi) is the expression, the wheel of existence itself. She is also the source of knowledge (Saraswati), bounty (Laxmi), and power (Kali) that enables the gods to create, sustain, and destroy.[3]

Most Hindus worship the divine either in the form of Vishnu (the Vaishnava tradition), Shiva (the Shaiva tradition), or Devi (the Shakta tradition). Vishnu, as sustainer, affirms worldly life by instituting and maintaining social order (dharma) in the manner of a cosmic king. Shiva, as destroyer, rejects all things worldly and manifests as the cosmic ascetic. Devi manifests herself either in a wild and independent form (Kali or Durga), or as a domesticated and submissive consort (Laxmi or Parvati), or as a shakti, an emanation of godly power embodied in female form. Brahma, the creator of the world of pleasure and pain, is generally ignored.[4]

Vishnu sustains the universe with the help of his consort Laxmi, goddess of wealth and fortune, a manifestation of Devi. Vishnu is visualized by artists as a blue-colored god (blue being the color of the sky, hence omnipresence), who bears in his four hands (stretching to the four corners of the universe) a conch (his trumpet that warns all wrongdoers to uphold the law), a discus (that ensures the cycle of life is maintained), a mace (his scepter with which he strikes law breakers), and a lotus (that beckons all creatures to enjoy the nectar of life). The goddess Laxmi is described as a beautiful lady dressed in a red sari (red being the color of fertility), bedecked with gems, holding a pot (a cornucopia) that overflows with gold and grain, seated on a lotus in a pond, flanked by white elephants (symbols of fertility, wealth and royal power) who consecrate her with water (symbol of the elixir of life). Vishnu, similar to the blue sky as he watches over the welfare of his consort, the red earth. She is the medium through which he expresses his divinity.

From time to time, whenever universal stability is threatened by disruptive forces, Vishnu descends from his heavenly abode, Vaikuntha, to set things right. He descends in many forms: sometimes animal, sometimes human, mostly male, occasionally female. Each time he restores order and returns to Vaikuntha.

MOHINI TRICKS BHASMA

Bhasma, the Asura, once pleased Shiva with his devotion and obtained the power to burn to ashes anyone on whose head he placed his hand. The Asura decided to try out his powers on Shiva himself. Shiva fled in terror and sought the help of Vishnu, who transformed into Mohini and distracted Bhasma. Overcome by lust, Bhasma begged Mohini to marry him. "Only if you dance like me," said Mohini. Bhasma agreed. During the course of her dance, Mohini touched her head. The deluded

Bhasma, blinded by desire, did this too and was burnt to ashes, much to the delight of Shiva.

Despite turning into a woman, Vishnu retains his male identity. His female form is more of disguise, making his actions a cross-dressing subterfuge. As a woman, he flirts, he charms, he overwhelms. The sexual transformation here must be contrasted from those in Chapter 2, where the transformed men lose memory of their former existence.

The previous story sheds light on the difference between Vishnu and Shiva. As a god who has to manage the affairs of the world, Vishnu uses not only force but also guile to get his way. The otherworldly Shiva, unused to the ways of the world, remains gullible (*bhola* in Hindi). So while the shrewd ever-smiling Vishnu is addressed as Mayin (the deluder), the serene simpleton Shiva is endearingly called Bholenath (the guileless one).

The story of how Mohini tricked Bhasma has made its way to Southeast Asia and forms the prelude of the *Thai Ramayana*.[5] In the *Ramakian* we learn how the four-armed Vishnu in the form of Mohini enchanted and killed a demon called Nontok, who misused the divine power bestowed upon him by Shiva. The demon accused him of beating him in an unfair fight. "You seduced me as a woman, then attacked me with four hands." So Vishnu decreed that in his next life Nontok would be reborn as the ten-armed Rakshasa-king Ravana, while he would take birth as a two-armed mortal man called Rama. "We will fight then and I will still defeat you." Thus, the epic becomes a preordained series of events molded by the laws of karma.

In Hindu lore, disruptive forces are often personified as *Asuras* and Rakshasas. There is no English word that can describe these harbingers of disorder perfectly. The word "demons" is more a convenient translation than a correct one, for demons are "evil beings" in a Christian construct, while "evil" as a concept has no place in Hindu world.[6]

Evil means the absence of godliness, but to a Hindu everything is a manifestation of the divine. In the *Bhagavad Gita*, when Krishna displays his cosmic form to Arjuna, he says. "I contain everything that is, was and will be. I am the source and destination of all." All characters in a Hindu narrative—even the demon and the villain—contain the spark of divinity. A Satan is not required to explain the undesirable actions since all events are accepted as reactions to past events. When demons defeat the gods, it is either because the gods are weakened by a curse or the demons are empowered by a boon.

Who then are the demons of Hinduism—the Asuras who are tricked by gods, the Rakshasas who are killed by heroes? They are, like the gods or Devas, the children of the creator, Brahma. The Puranas state that at the dawn of the cosmos, the primal mage Kashyapa, a manifestation of the self-created Brahma, fathered on his many wives various creatures that populate the cosmos. Thus he became Prajapati, lord of progeny. One of his wives, known as Aditi, gave birth to the Adityas. The Adityas reside in the celestial realms known as Swarga (mistranslated as heaven) and are keepers of light, hence known as Devas (div = light in Sanskrit). This word Devas is commonly mistranslated as "gods" (deus = god in Latin).

Another wife, Diti, gave birth to the Daityas. The Daityas reside in the nether regions known as Patala (mistranslated as hell), are devoid of sap and hence known as Asuras (according to the Mahabharata, a = no; sura = sap, elixir, ambrosia). These Asuras become "demons" in popular English translations of Hindu lore—such as the comic book series Amar Chitra Katha—on grounds that they are eternal enemies of the gods hence, as the Western discourse informs us, evil.

To reduce the battle of the Devas and the Asuras as the eternal battle of good and evil is to reduce Hindu lore into a convenient Occidental dualism. The antagonism eludes such simplistic explanations, since both parties are children of Brahma, and all of them are divine. Many Asuras and Rakshasas are revered as devotees of Bhagavan (for example, the Asura-prince, Prahalad, is a devotee of Vishnu while the Rakshasa-king, Ravana, is a devotee of Shiva) and are even considered worthy of worship (for example, the Asura-king, Bali, is worshipped in the state of Kerala because he rises from his subterranean realm along with the harvest).

Both Devas and Asuras play crucial roles in churning out the goddess Laxmi from the ocean of milk as the following story from the *Puranas* informs us. The many retellings of the story can be found in the book *Goddess Lakshmi: Origin and Development* by Upendra Nath Dhal.

MOHINI FOOLS THE ASURAS

Great treasures lay dissolved in the ocean of milk. The Adityas wanted to churn them out. They sought the help of Vishnu who advised them to seek the cooperation of their half-brothers, the

Daityas, since such a grand endeavor could be realized only with their support. Together they set up a giant churn, using Meru, king of the mountains, as the spindle and Vasuki, king of the serpents, as the churning rope. Garuda, king of the birds and Vishnu's mount carried the churn to the ocean. It would have sunk but at the crucial moment, Akupara, king of the turtles and an incarnation of Vishnu, came to the rescue. He held the churn on his mighty back. The Daityas then caught the head-end of the serpent-king while the Adityas caught the neck-end of the serpent-king and began churning. The churning went on for eons. Finally, the milky ocean coagulated and revealed its secrets. Out came many wonderful things: a wish-fulfilling tree called Kalpataru; a dream-realizing gem called Chintamani; a cow whose udder was always full of milk called Kamadhenu; a bow that never missed its mark called Saranga; a seven-headed horse that always rode into victory called Ucchaishrava; an unstoppable royal white-skinned, six-tusked elephant called Airavata; and finally, Laxmi, the goddess of wealth and fortune, who chose Vishnu as her husband. At long last emerged a pot containing the elixir of immortality— Amrita. The Daityas grabbed it and ran away. The Adityas appealed to Vishnu, who took the form of the celestial enchantress Mohini and approached the Daityas, titillating them with her sensuous walk. "May I serve the divine liquid," she asked flirtatiously. The Asuras, bewitched by her beauty, could not refuse. They gave her the pot. So besotted were they by her sultry smile and her voluptuous figure that they failed to notice she was distributing the Amrita only amongst the Adityas. The Daitya Rahu suspected the intentions of this damsel and sat amongst the Adityas as one of them. Just as he was about to take a sip of the elixir, the sun and the moon recognized him and alerted Mohini. She hurled a discus, cut Rahu's throat, and prevented the divine liquid from entering the Daitya's body. The other Daityas realized Vishnu had duped them. They declared war on the Adityas. Led by Vishnu, the Adityas drove the Daityas to the nether realms. Then, laying claim over all the treasures that emerged from the ocean of milk, the Adityas rose to the celestial realm where they set up their city, Amravati, the city of the immortals.

By consuming the elixir of immortality, the Adityas conquer death. Surrounded by the treasures of the ocean, they become resplendent guardians of light and fertility, hence Devas. Devoid of the divine drink, the Daityas transform into Asura and are forced to seek refuge in the nether regions. But the Asuras are not quite mortal. Their preceptor, the sage Shukra, does possess the secret of reviving the dead (see Chapter 2). Thus the Devas and Asuras are evenly matched and the two constantly fight for control over the cosmos.

Most narrations begin with the Asuras—empowered by boons earned by austerities that please Brahma—overwhelming the Devas. They end with the Devas—championed by Vishnu, Shiva, or Devi— striking back and reclaiming their city. The Asuras are in control when the Devas are weak: at night, in the waning half of the moon, when the tides ebb, and in the colder, darker half of the year. The battles are constant and the results impermanent. The vacillating fortunes ensures the cyclical ebb and flow of cosmic energy that brings about a predictable dynamism in the cycle of life.

At no point do Devas forget that Mohini is Vishnu. The word Mohini, meaning delusion personified, comes from the root moha— enchantment. A weak and unenlightened mind, embodied in the Daitya, fails to discover the truth of Vishnu and is seduced by Mohini. Thus another attribute of Hindu demons is their inability to recognize the divine. This, the scriptures imply, results from ignorance, egoism, and their earthbound state. Their subterranean abode is even farther away—when compared to the world of humans—from the celestial realms of knowledge and truth.

According to Hindu cosmology, the universe is a vertical structure with the spirit on top and matter below.[7] The less attached we are to earthbound pleasure the more Deva-like we become and ascend to celestial realms; the more attached we are to worldly things the more Asura-like we become and sink to the lower chthonian realms. Looking at the narrative as an allegory, there are Devas and Asuras within us and Mohinis around us. It is up to us to not to succumb to the charm of Mohini, recognize the divine truth, and obtain a sip of Amrita. Only then will we possess that which liberates us from the transitory pleasures and pains of mundane existence.

In a less-known tale of Mohini from the *Ganesha Purana* (900-1400 C.E.), retold in Vettam Mani's *Puranic Encyclopaedia,* we learn how even the wise Virochana succumbed to the charms of Mohini and lost his crown (his head, his intelligence?).

MOHINI KILLS VIROCHANA

Virochana, king of the Asuras, was given a magic crown by the sun-god Surya. As long as the crown rested on his head, no one could harm him. So Vishnu took the form of Mohini, enchanted Virochana, and stole his crown. Without the protection of the crown, Virochana was vulnerable to all weapons. Vishnu took advantage of this and killed him.

In the next story, it is not demons, but sages who are enchanted by Mohini. This story is essentially a Shaiva lore, but here Vishnu joins Shiva to teach the pompous sages a lesson. This retelling takes away the homoerotic twist where both women and men are aroused by Shiva's beauty. In this narrative, the sages and their wives are forced to confront their weaknesses. They might know magical rituals that give them great external power but these prove valueless in the absence of inner strength. This story comes from *Skanda Purana* and has been retold in Wendy Dongier O'Flaherty's *Shiva: The Erotic Ascetic,* and in the Amar Chitra Katha comic book *Elephanta.*

MOHINI ENCHANTS THE SAGES

A group of sages performed rituals in the forest and believed themselves to be as powerful as the gods. To humble them, Shiva and Vishnu entered this forest in the guise of a handsome beggar called Bhikshatan and a beautiful maid called Mohini. The sages and their wives saw this couple and were overwhelmed with desire. The men ran after Mohini while the women chased Bhikshatan. Some time later, they regained control of their senses and held Bhikshatan and Mohini responsible for the momentary lapse in their reason. Using their magic powers, they drew out of fire a serpent, a lion, an elephant, and a goblin. Shiva picked up the serpent and wound it round his neck. He flayed the lion and the elephant and wrapped their skins round his body. He then jumped on the goblins back and began to dance, displaying his divine splendor. The sages watched spellbound and realized their folly.

During the Brahmotsavam festivities, when Vishnu's image is bedecked as Mohini, the devotee is presented with the female form of the lord, the incarnation that enchants and deludes the greedy power-hungry Asuras and the egotistical sages. The devotee is exhorted to look beyond the appearances that delude (Mohini) into the reality that liberates (Vishnu).

Mohini is the family deity of Gauda Saraswat Brahmins, who refer to her as "Shri Mahalasa Narayani."[8] Though the deity is viewed as female and is worshipped as a manifestation of the mother-goddess, the devotee is constantly reminded that the goddess is in essence a form of Vishnu. Thus gender fluidity is prevalent in viewing the divine, which imparts the shrine with mystery and sacredness. Sociological readings into the worship of Mahalasa-devi suggest a conscious attempt to reconcile rival Hindu theistic schools—the Shaktas and the Vaishnavas.

This need for syncretism is common in Hinduism, and it is achieved symbolically by fusing the identities of various deities through sexual union. The following story from the *Shiva Purana* does just that. It has been retold in Wendy Doniger O'Flaherty's *Shiva: The Erotic Ascetic*.

VISHNU AROUSES SHIVA

When Vishnu transformed into Mohini, the celestial enchantress, Shiva was so overwhelmed with desire that he abandoned his consort Parvati and ran after Mohini until he had shed his seed. From this seed was born the mighty monkey-god Hanuman, who the gods decreed would vanquish demons and even death. As foretold, Hanuman helped Rama rescue his wife Sita from the clutches of the Rakshasa-king Ravana.

In medieval times, there was great rivalry between the worshippers of Shiva and Vishnu traditions. Each one approached life differently: the Shaivas saw value in the ascetic tradition while Vaishnavas upheld the householder tradition. Philosophical and ritualistic differences sometimes led to violent confrontations. Gods such as Hanuman helped bridge the gap. Hanuman is born of Shiva, but Vishnu inspires his birth. Hanuman's lifestyle (celibacy) and personality (humility and innocence rising from wisdom) endorse Shaiva philosophy; his cosmic role (fighting demons, helping people) reflects Vaishnava ideas. Thus is the union of two rival orders achieved.

The spilling of a sage's seed at the sight of a nymph or Apsara is a recurring theme in Hindu lore. Apsaras are celestial courtesans who sing, dance, and entertain the gods. Sages determined to gain power over the elements, and hence Devas, control the five senses and perform austerities. To thwart their ambition, the Devas recruit the aid of Apsaras. More often than not, the sages succumb to the charm of sultry nymphs and shed semen. But, the nymphs failed miserably when they tried to enchant Shiva. When their patron, the love-god Kama, dared shoot his love-dart at the hermit-god, Shiva opened his third eye, let loose a fiery missile, and reduced Kama to ashes. Realizing Shiva was no ordinary sage, the Devas—who desperately needed a warlord born of Shiva's seed—invoked the mother-goddess. She took the form of the mountain princess Parvati and won Shiva's heart through austerities. Though the two unite, they never conceive a child together. Metaphysically, this means spirit and matter retain distinct identities. Shiva and Parvati create children autonomously. Kartikeya is born of Shiva's seed but not nurtured in Parvati's womb (see Chapter 2) and Ganesha is born not of Shiva's seed but of rubbings of Parvati's skin (see Chapter 5).

Mohini personifies yet another attempt to make Shiva worldly. Since Apsaras are no match for Shiva, Vishnu takes on the role of the enchantress. On the walls of the Mattencheri palace in Kerala is a mural of Shiva embracing Mohini passionately while Parvati, Shiva's consort, watches their interaction with a resigned smirk. She knows her husband is a simpleton and a hemp smoker, his otherworldliness stemming from his sublimation of all constructs. She understands his fascination for Mohini and his entanglement in Vishnu's enchanting web. Maybe he is too inebriated to know Mohini is Vishnu. Maybe he does not care. Either way, the goal is reached and Shiva enters the cycle of life.

Of course, only Vishnu has the power to enchant Shiva, by becoming a woman. When a demon tried to do the same, he failed miserably.

DEATH OF ADI

The demon Adi wanted to kill Shiva. Once, taking advantage of Parvati's absence, he took her form and gained entry into Shiva's abode. When Shiva expressed his desire to make love, Adi placed sharp teeth in his vagina. Shiva divined that the woman in his arm was not his consort but an imposter, but he continued with the charade to teach Adi a lesson. He placed a thunderbolt on his manhood, and penetrated Adi. Realizing his game was up, the demon tried to wriggle out of Shiva's embrace but failed. He was forced to endure the fatal lovemaking.

The *Agni Purana* (c. 850 C.E.) states that after the seed is shed, Shiva recovers his senses, becomes cool, and turns back from this improper conduct act.[9] It is never made clear whether the improper act is losing control of his senses or being seduced by one who is not quite a woman. Since Mohini is in essence a male god (and Adi is a male demon) Vishnu, many people have pointed to the blatant homoeroticism here. But is the homoeroticism here crucial or just incidental? Focusing only on the homoeroticism tends to take all the attention away from the narrative's deeper metaphysical significance.

In Hindu lore, womanhood has always personified worldly mundane life. When Vishnu becomes a woman, he embodies the pleasures and responsibilities of a householder's life. The aim of his enchanting subterfuge is to entice the transcendent Shiva into samsara. As the god who exhorts all creatures to be part of worldly life, Vishnu finds his greatest challenge in the hermit-god. Shiva resolutely refuses to be part of the world, meditating stubbornly on the icy peaks of Mount Kailas. The two manifestations of godhead embody opposing approaches to life. Vishnu wants to participate in the mundane life *(pravritti marga)*, Shiva wants to stay away from it *(nivritti marga)*. The seduction aims to resolve this antagonism by transforming the hermit into the householder, or at least, enchanting him to the point that he does not transcend worldliness completely.

As discussed in Chapter 1, according to Hindu occult sciences known as Tantra, when semen is retained it helps man break free from the cycle of life; when it is spilt it entraps man in it. Shaiva lore revolves around the desperate attempts of gods to make Shiva shed seed and become worldly. In Chapter 2, the Devas beseech him to spill his semen and father the divine warlord Kartikeya, who will defeat the Asuras. In the *Agni Purana* it is said that drops of Shiva's semen, which fell to the ground as he followed Mohini, became lingas (Shiva aniconic emblems). His symbols thus become earthbound. The semen spilt at the sight of Mohini generates the virile warrior-god Hanuman, a god who helps Vishnu fight disruptive social forces and establishes dharma.

The story of Shiva spilling his seed at the sight of Mohini also explains the origin of Ayyappa, the god enshrined at Sabarimalai in

Kerala. Ayyappa is also known as Manikantha and Hari-Hara-suta
(the son of Hari or Vishnu and Hara or Shiva). Ayyappa also unites
Shaiva and Vaishnava traditions. He is a vira, the virile warrior-monk
who shuns material pleasures, avoids women, fights demons, and
lives like a yogi. The following story of Ayyappa is partly based on
the *Brahmanda Purana* and partly on folklore. Retellings can be
found in the Amar Chitra Katha comic book *Ayyappa,* in Wendy
Doniger's *Splitting the Difference,* Alain Danielou's *Gods of Love and
Ecstasy,* and in *Same-Sex Love in India* edited by Ruth Vanita and
Saleem Kidwai.

THE SON OF SHIVA AND VISHNU

Shiva once saw Vishnu in the form of Mohini. Overwhelmed by
desire he embraced Mohini and spilt his semen. From the spilt
seed was born a child who was given into the care of a childless
king. The boy was called Manikantha, because at birth he had a
jeweled bell round his neck. The boy grew up to be a wise,
brave, and virile warrior who defended his kingdom from ma-
rauders, winning the love and respect of the people. During his
quest, he befriended a Muslim warrior called Vavar and low-
caste warrior called Kadutha. Meanwhile, Manikantha's foster
mother, the queen, became pregnant and she gave birth to a son.
Suddenly ambition reared its ugly head. The queen wanted her
son, not the adopted Manikantha, to succeed her husband. To
get rid of the rival, she feigned illness and claimed that only ti-
ger's milk collected by a chaste youth would cure her. Manikantha
immediately set out on the mission. He tamed the tigers with his
divine aura, milked the tigress, and made his journey back to the
palace on tigers. On the way, he met an ogress called Mahishi,
who challenged him to a fight. Manikantha fought and killed
her. From the corpse emerged a nymph called Leela. She had
been cursed that she would wander in the forest as an ogress until a chaste young man defeated her in battle. She begged
Manikantha to marry her. "I will," he said, "the day no chaste
young man visits my shrine." Manikantha returned to his father's kingdom seated on tigers, cheered by the people. He gave
the queen the milk she wanted and then, having divine her true
intention, renounced the crown, took shelter atop Mount
Sabarimalai, and began to meditate. The king begged him to re-

turn, but he refused. Not wanting to lose his son, the king tied a piece of cloth around Manikantha's legs and had a shrine built to his glory atop Mount Sabarimalai. Eighteen steps led to this shrine, indicating the eighteen years Manikantha spent as a prince before transforming into a divine being, a chaste warrior, a vira, a god. People called the boy-god Ayyappa (father).

The birth of Ayyappa is not biological. Mohini/Vishnu does not get pregnant; he merely arouses Shiva to spill the seed. Ayyappa is thus a ayonija vira, a nonwomb-born hero. As explained in Chapter 2, semen aroused by austerities and restraint becomes so powerful that it can transform into a pure male child on its own without the intervention of the female seed or the incubation provided by the womb.

The story of Manikantha/Ayyappa does have misogynist and (hence?) homoerotic undertones. The enemies of the hero are two women (the queen and the ogress). He shuns the company of women, avoids marriage, and prefers the company of men, especially his warrior friends (a Muslim and a low-caste warrior)[10] and his chaste male devotees. These traits make sense within the context of the eternal Hindu conflict between this-worldly desires and otherworldly aspirations. As a vira, Ayyappa's spiritual power lies in his chastity and continence. By opposing women who personify worldly ambition (the queen) and Nature's unbridled sex and violence (the nymph and the ogress), Ayyappa leans toward monasticism and otherworldly aspirations. He symbolizes freedom from the transient earthly pleasure and embodies eternal spiritual bliss. Of course, as with all things Hindu, this is not absolutely true, for there are satellite shrines of Ayyappa where he is depicted as a married man with two wives— Poorna and Pushkala (as at Achankovil).[11]

Sociologically speaking, the cult of Ayyappa unites not only Shaiva and Vaishnava, but also Shakta traditions. The nymph (Mahishi's alter ego) who waits to marry Ayyappa in enshrined in the temple of Malikapurathamma on a nearby hill, as his shakti, power personified.[12] Further by linking Ayyappa to a Muslim and to Kadhutha, a conscious attempt is made to bring together Hindus and Muslims as well as upper- and lower-castes Hindus. Pilgrims to Sabarimalai are obliged to pay a visit to a mosque dedicated in memory of Vavar before visiting Ayyappa's shrine. In the main shrine, Ayyappa is a celibate yogi, so no woman of fertile age is allowed to visit the shrine.

Only men, purified after weeks of fasting, prayer, and continence, can climb the mountain and surrender themselves to Ayyappa's grace.

Ayyappa's nonassociation with women is, in a sense, nonassociation with the cycle of birth and death. Ayyappa embodies immortality. As a result, when Ayyappa replaces Brahma as the creator-god, he takes advantage of his new position to bestow immortality on all his devotees, angering the gods. This story comes from a Kannada song referred to in the book *Same-Sex Love in India*. The mischief-making sage Narada saves the day by asking Ayyappa, "If Shiva is your father and Vishnu is your mother, then how are you related to Shiva's wife Parvati and Vishnu's wife Lakshmi?" Unable to answer the question, Ayyappa abandons his role as creator, renounces heaven, and returns to earth. The story captures the tension stemming from the idea that Ayyappa is the offspring of two male deities, no matter what the sociological subtext.

The trend of using gender metamorphosis and sexual union to achieve syncretism is also seen in the following story from the *Mahabhagvata Purana* (c. 1100 C.E.), a text from Bengal. Wendy Doniger O'Flaherty refers to it in her essay "Androgynes" in her book *Sexual Metaphors and Animal Symbols in Indian Mythology*.

KALI BECOMES KRISHNA

At the behest of the Devas, the goddess Kali descended upon earth as Krishna, the cowherd, to rid the earth of ambitious kings. Shiva prayed to Kali and was permitted to descend as Radha, Krishna's consort, in order to make love in reverse, with her in the dominate position. Thus, Shiva and Kali were together on earth as they were on Mount Kailas.

In Bengal, Vaishnava and Shakta traditions manifest as the worship of Krishna and Kali. Both traditions dominated life and were equally respected for centuries, creating a deep need for making these theistic schools complementary, especially in view of the contrasting paradigms associated with either deity. While Krishna is a winsome, shrewd, and vegetarian cowherd-god who makes women dance to his tunes in meadows, Kali is the wild, autonomous, and blood-thirsty killer-goddess who stands naked on her consort Shiva while he lies prone on the ground. Differences are reconciled when Kali (female) manifests as Krishna (male), and Shiva (male) becomes Radha (female). As Radha, Shiva gets to sit on Kali and make love in reverse. Sexual transformation enables the devotee to relate to two deities as one.

Another story attempts to reconcile the worship of Shiva in the city of Krishna, through gender metamorphosis. This story is unique because it is one of the few where Shiva becomes a woman (hence subordinate to the presiding deity of the city). It was narrated to me by Ann Kim, who was doing research in Mathura, the holy city of Krishna, on the banks of the river Yamuna in northern India. She informed me that the story has been retold in *Journey Through the Twelve Forests* by David L. Haberman and referred to briefly in A. W. Entwistle's *Braj, Centre of Krishna Pilgrimage*. Braj, or Vraja, the land around Mathura on the banks of the river Yamuna, is associated with the life of Krishna. The story is a *Sthala Purana,* a chronicle related to a particular shrine, with no other scriptural testimony. It relates to a small temple of Shiva on the banks of the Yamuna, where the sacred linga stone is dressed every night as a *gopi*, or milkmaid, in the privacy of the sanctum sanctorum.

SHIVA, THE MILKMAID

Every night the milkmaids of Vraja would circle Krishna and dance in the meadows of Madhuvana while he played the flute. This was the mystical dance of union with the supreme divine principle known as Maharaas. Shiva, enchanted by the splendor of this dance, decided to participate in it. He arrived on the banks of the Yamuna along with Parvati. Parvati joined the sacred dance, but Shiva was prevented from entering the magic circle because he was a man. In the Maharaas, only Krishna was male, everyone else was female. Determined to join the Maharaas, Shiva bathed in the river Yamuna and the river-goddess transformed him into a woman. In this female form, Shiva entered the magic circle and began to dance. As the dance continued into the night, the milkmaids noticed that Krishna gave more attention to the new arrival. Krishna's favorite Radha demanded an explanation. "He is Shiva, the supreme cosmic dancer, my teacher. I dance with him for him." The milkmaids saluted Shiva and watched, spellbound, the divine dance of Nataraja (Shiva, the dancer) and Natwara (Krishna, the dancer).

As with Mohini, Krishna is an incarnation of Vishnu. But unlike other incarnations, Krishna has superceded even Vishnu in popularity to the extent that he is considered the perfect earthly manifestation of Vishnu, the only form through which Vishnu can be understood, approached, and realized. Throughout the ages, Krishna has been visualized as a adorable child, a winsome prankster, a loving son, a charming flautist, an enchanting rake, a caring friend, a delightful lover, a noble husband, a fierce warrior, a wise philosopher, a determined diplomat, a wily strategist, and an awesome god. It is said that even to visualize Krishna as a manipulative enemy is a form of devotion, for enmity causes one to think of Krishna so many times that one ends up blessed.[13]

For Hindus, just as the word Shiva evokes serenity and the word Vishnu evokes awe, the word Krishna evokes love, all kinds of love, from the sublime to the sensuous. In the worship of Krishna, devotees are told to love the divine in human terms, considering the lord to be either their child, friend, teacher, master, or lover. To look upon Krishna as one's divine lover is not difficult in view of the unabashed erotic form attributed to him—gentle face, curly hair, dark skin, welcoming eyes, mysterious smile, lithe limbs, bedecked with yellow silk, jewels, peacock feather, bright garlands, and sandal paste. In Krishna, the spiritual and the erotic cannot be differentiated.

Love for Krishna has led some male devotees to reject their masculinity so that just as Shiva became a milkmaid to join the Maharaas, they too get a chance to join their divine beloved in the mystical dance. These devotees wear female apparel, behave like women, and call themselves Sakhis, companions of Radha, Krishna's beloved milkmaid. In their reverence for Radha, they do not identify themselves with her. By identifying themselves as her handmaidens they believe they will get greater access to the lord.[14] It is interesting to note that unlike other religious orders where the male biology is considered essential for liberation from the cycle of life, the order of Sakhis insist on rejecting the male identity in order to break free from material reality and merge with the divine. Not that this practice is appreciated. Commenting on them in his book *Vaisnavism, Saivism and Minor Religious Systems,* R. G. Bhandarkar has said,

> Their appearances and acts are so disgusting that they do not show themselves very much in public, and their number is small

... They deserve notice here only to show that, when the female element is idolized and made the object of special worship, such disgusting corruptions must ensue.[15]

Krishna was born to rid the kings whose greed and ambitions burdened the earth. The story goes that the earth-goddess approached Vishnu in the form of a cow and begged him to save her: the ambitions of man was breaking her back and greed was making her udders sore. Vishnu agreed to descend on earth as Krishna and rid her of the burden. Keeping this story in mind, an explanation given for homosexuality by a Tamil Vaishnava Brahmin acquires great significance. His views appear in Shakuntala Devi's book *The World of Homosexuals*. According to him, the rapid growth in human population and the decline in animal population has burdened the earth and created a cosmic imbalance. Birth of humans who naturally veer away from procreative practices (e.g. same-sex desiring men and women) is Nature's way of controlling unchecked human fertility.[16]

Krishna was raised amongst cowherds and he grew up protecting his cows and his village from demons. As a child, he raided dairies, stole butter, and endeared himself into the hearts of the milkmaids with his mischief. As a youth, he enchanted the women with his smile, his music, and his dance. Every full-moon night, he would go to the beautiful meadow known as Madhuvana, on the banks of the Yamuna, and play the flute. The music roused love in the hearts of the milkmaids who would run to Madhuvana, circle Krishna, and dance to his tune. This was no ordinary dance; this was the Maharaas, the dance of mystical union. Here, Krishna was the guiding spirit, consciousness itself, while the women embodied the particles that make up material reality. They moved rhythmically to the tune of Krishna's music until there was no difference between the dance and the music, and the dancer and the musician. All became one.

The Maharaas is open only to women. Krishna is the only man. For men to gain entry into it, they have to become women. In the previous story, Shiva becomes a milkmaid to dance with Krishna. The *Padma Purana* narrates a similar story about Arjuna. The story has been translated and compiled in the book *Same-Sex Love in India*. Similar to Shiva, when Arjuna expresses his desire to participate in Krishna's mystical dance, he is first transformed into a woman and then given entry. As with Shiva, the sexual transformation occurs after a dip in

the river. Arjuna experiences that which no man has expe
is exhorted by Krishna not to share his secret encounter v

The Maharaas always takes place at night, outside the .
secret. There is something magical and clandestine about it, to .
breaks free from all social norms. It is an event where all boundaries
are broken, all identities shattered. It is a return to primal innocence
when love reigns alone and everything else is cast aside. The women
leave their husbands and risk dishonor as they come to Krishna. Yet
they come, for Krishna is the divine who can be attained only when
one sheds all pretenses and facades. During the day, in the village, the
milkmaids live as ordinary women do, as wives, sisters, and daughters, upholding social values. At night, in the wilderness, they shed
social identities, become free women, and dance unashamedly into
the arms of the lord. Thus the conflict between cultural demands and
natural urges are reconciled. The two coexist. Both the inherent freedom of life and the necessary repression by society accept and respect one another.

Of all the milkmaids, there was one who was very dear to Krishna.
She was Radha. In one tradition, the *parakiya parampara,* Radha is
said to be older to him and the wife of Krishna's maternal uncle. Thus
the relationship is adulterous, incestuous, and unconventional (older
woman, younger man).[17] This tradition sometimes insists that Radha's
husband was impotent and her secret meeting with Krishna was a
meeting with her true (divine) husband (thus attempting to downplay
the adultery). In the Bengal tradition discussed earlier, where Krishna
is identified with Kali and Shiva with Radha, Shiva asks Kali to make
his earthly husband impotent, thus preventing his violation even in
his female form. In another tradition, the *svakiya parampara,* that
considers even the suggestion of adultery and incest blasphemy,
Radha is Krishna's mystical wife, a manifestation of his delight, born
when Krishna looked into the mirror and experienced desire.[18] The
yearning of Radha for Krishna is said to be an allegory for the yearning of the individual soul for the divine. This idea is brought out in the
following story based on the medieval devotional poetry.

KRISHNA WEARS RADHA'S CLOTHES

Every night Radha would risk everything to be with Krishna.
She would slip out of her house in the middle of the night and

make her way through the woods to the meadows of Madhuvana
on the banks of the river Yamuna, where Krishna would play the
flute and enchant her with his winsome smile and passionate
embrace. In her love for Krishna, Radha would sometimes be
jealous, possessive, or quarrelsome. She felt that Krishna would
never understand her anguish and longing until he could become her. So to pacify Radha, Krishna decided that one night
they should exchange roles. At the appointed hour, Krishna wore
Radha's clothes and Radha wore Krishna's clothes. She played
the flute and he danced around her. She took the lead when they
made love and occupied the active position. She dominated him.
"Even then, Krishna, you cannot understand me," Radha told
her beloved, "You can dress like me, talk and dance like me, but
you can never feel what I feel for we can never exchange
hearts."

By becoming Radha, Krishna makes the ultimate declaration of
his love. This episode has inspired rituals, such as the secret ceremony in Nathadvara where Krishna-Srinathji is dressed as a woman.
No one but the participating priest has seen the image of Srinathji
dressed as a woman. One painting of this form of the lord can be seen
in Amit Ambalal's book on Rajasthani paintings from Nathdvara,
Krishna As Srinathji. Ambalal informs us that the painting was done
based on descriptions given by the head of the temple, Govardhanlalji,
since no one else had actually seen the apparel. After the painting was
done in the early twentieth century, Govardhanlalji issued a ban on
painters, forbidding them to depict Srinathji as a woman.

The image of Krishna dressed as Radha captures the inherent
tensions between spiritual and material reality, between man and
woman, between actuality and appearance, between representation
and reality, between sex and gender, between culture and nature.
Though Krishna and Radha exchange clothes and sexual roles, the
essential biological differences remain. At dawn, Radha must wear a
woman's clothes, behave like a woman, leave the wilderness of natural law, and return to the village under the mantle of social law.

Krishna's life as the pivot of the Maharaas comes to an abrupt end
when duty beckons him to the city of Mathura. In an instant, he turns
away from the bucolic joys of the village and enters the wicked world
of urbane politics. He gives up Radha and his flute. The romance of
Madhuvan loses priority as the corruption of Mathura reveals itself.

Krishna, the lover, must become Krishna, the restorer of dharma. The milkmaids cry and beg him to stay. Krishna leaves nevertheless. He has to, for the playful god is also detachment personified.

The early part of Krishna's life was first described in the *Harivamsa* and the rest forms part of the epic *Mahabharata*. The most important retelling of Krishna's life is the *Bhagavata Purana,* but information that is closest to most followers comes from devotional songs and stories composed through the ages. In them we learn how, after leaving the village of cowherds, Krishna joins forces with the Pandavas and sets about destroying the wicked kings of earth, resorting more often than not to guile and subterfuge. The following story of how Krishna, in his quest to establish dharma, defeated a demon by becoming a woman is told by the Alis of Tamil Nadu, and has been retold by Wendy Doniger in her book *Splitting the Difference.*

KRISHNA KILLS ARAKA

The demon Araka had never laid eyes on a woman. His chastity made him invulnerable. One day he met a beautiful woman called Mohini and was overwhelmed by desire. Three days after this incident, Krishna met Araka in battle and succeeded in killing him. Krishna revealed to the gods that Mohini was one of his many forms. He declared that in the age of darkness, Kali Yuga, there will be many more creatures who are neither male nor female and whatever words come from their mouths, whether good or bad, will come true.

It is clear that in the previous story, the narrators do not differentiate between Vishnu and Krishna. This trend is common in folklore. The story does not make it clear whether the transformation is biological or merely cosmetic. A similar plot is found in the following narrative where Krishna and his companion, the Pandava Arjuna, become women to trick a sorcerer. The tale comes from northern districts of Tamil Nadu where Draupadi, the common wife of the Pandavas (see Chapter 1) is worshipped as a manifestation of the mother-goddess. The many variants of this story have been retold in Alf Hiltebeitel's *The Cult of Draupadi.*

KRISHNA AND ARJUNA
AS MOTHER AND DAUGHTER

A sorcerer possessed five sacred objects that the Pandavas needed to defeat their enemies, the Kauravas. He lived in an impregnable fort and could be killed by none other than his son. Krishna and Arjuna came up with a plan to kill the sorcerer, destroy his fort, and acquire the sacred objects. Krishna disguised himself as an old woman while Arjuna bedecked himself as a ravishing maiden named Vijayampal. They approached the sorcerer's son Pormannan, introducing themselves as mother and daughter. Enchanted by Vijayampal's looks, Pormannan sought her hand in marriage. "If you want to marry her, you must kill your father, destroy his fort and bring us the five sacred objects, he possesses," said Krishna. Pormannan, overwhelmed by desire, killed his father, destroyed the fort, stole the sacred objects, and ran after Krishna and Arjuna. When he discovered they were not women, he was angry. "Who will satisfy my desire now?" he asked. Feeling sorry for the youth, the Pandavas let him marry their sister and made him a senior officer in their army.

Though not explicit, Arjuna and Krishna are clearly involved in a cross-dressing subterfuge. They become women to seduce the villain to his destruction. The question may be raised, "Why did they not use a woman instead?" The frustrated Pormannan is so aroused by Vijayampal's beauty that he demands satisfaction. Any woman will do. Thus any suggestion of a same-sex union between the hero and the villain is cast aside. The hero may seduce the villain, but he does not sleep with him.

In the following story from a folk retelling of the *Mahabharata,* cross-dressing helps another Pandava win the day. The story involves Arjuna's son Abhimanyu and Bhima's son Ghatotkacha. One version of the story can be found in the Amar Chitra Katha comic book, *Ghatotkacha.*

GHATOTKACHA IN WOMEN'S CLOTHES

Krishna belonged to the Yadava clan that had close ties with the Kuru clan. Unfortunately, the Kuru clan had split into the

Kauravas and the Pandavas. Krishna wanted the Yadavas to support the Pandavas, but his elder brother, Balarama, sided with the Kauravas. To establish a strong alliance with the Kauravas, Balarama decided that his sister, Subhadra, should be given in marriage to the eldest Kaurava Duryodhan. Krishna did not support this and helped Subhadra elope with Arjuna, the Pandava. Years later, Balarama decided to give his daughter Vatsala in marriage to Duryodhana's son Laxman. Vatsala, however, wanted to marry her Aunt Subhadra's son Abhimanyu. Not only did Balarama refuse, he posted guards to prevent her from eloping. Desperate, Vatsala sent word to Abhimanyu, who sought the help of his half brother Ghatotkacha, King of Rakshasas. On the day of the wedding, Ghatotkacha flew into Balarama's palace, cast a spell of sleep, and carried Vatsala off to his mountain abode where Abhimanyu was waiting for her. Ghatatkocha then returned to Balarama's palace, transformed himself into the very likeness of Vatsala, and took the place of the real Vatsala so that she would not be missed. During the wedding ceremony, when Balarama gave his daughter's hand to Laxmana, Ghatotkacha squeezed the groom's hand with such force that he fainted. Then revealing his true form, he laughed at the assembled guests and flew away.

As with his son Ghatotkacha, Bhima too is involved in a cross-dressing subterfuge. This event occurs during the final year of the Pandava exile following the loss of their kingdom to the Kauravas in a game of dice. The story is found in all popular retellings of the epic.

BHIMA IN WOMEN'S CLOTHES

In the thirteenth year of their exile, when they were obliged to live incognito, the five Pandavas took shelter in the court of King Virata. The noble Yudhishtira, the mighty Bhima, the archer Arjuna, the handsome Nakula, and the wise Sahadeva disguised themselves as a priest, a cook, a eunuch dancer, a stable hand, and a cowherd. Their common-wife Draupadi disguised herself as a palace maid named Sairandhri and gained employment in the quarters of Virata's queen Sudeshna. The queen treated her kindly. After about ten months, the queen's brother Kichaka, who was also the commander-in-chief, saw Draupadi and, being enamored by her beauty, made sexual overtures toward her. When she turned him down, he refused to give up.

Overwhelmed by desire, he forced his sister to send Draupadi to his quarters on the pretext of collecting wine. There he tried to rape Draupadi but she managed to give him the slip. She ran to the king and begged protection. But, the king feared his mighty brother-in-law. He did nothing as Kichaka ran into the court, caught Draupadi by the hair, and beat her in public. Even Yudhishtira, who sat next to the king, did nothing for fear of giving away his identity, an act that would have forced the Pandavas to remain in exile for another thirteen years. Bristling with fury, Draupadi went to Bhima, who served in the palace kitchens and demanded that he do his duty as a husband. Together they hatched a plan. Draupadi sent a message to Kichaka asking him to meet her in a lonely corner of the theater at night. Bhima waited for him disguised as a woman. When Kichaka arrived, he mistook Bhima for Draupadi and approached lustfully. Bhima returned his embrace with such force that Kichaka was crushed to a pulp.

The story of the death of Kichaka is a popular theme in plays and ballets. The plot of mighty Bhima dressed up as a woman seducing Kichaka and then "wrestling" him to death is seen as comedic. At no point does his cross-dressing cast aspersions on his sexual orientation. Cross-dressing is acceptable as long as it helps kill villains and save damsels. When it supports anything other than a heterosexual agenda, it meets with hostility, as suggested in the following story compiled by Ki. Rajanarayanan of Pondichevry and narrated to me by C. S. Lakshmi.[19] It is the story of a folk goddess from Tamil Nadu. What follows is my understanding of the narrative.

SANTOSHI AND HER BROTHER

A king once saw a beautiful girl in the fields. Overwhelmed by desire, he ordered her to come to the royal garden at night bedecked as a bride. To save her honor, her twin brother went in her place dressed as a woman. The sister saw the king make love to her brother. The two seemed to be enjoying it. Even a dog who stood nearby was excited by what was happening. Angered by the turn of events, she transformed into a fiery goddess, raised her sword, killed the king, her brother, and even the dog, and took refuge in the forest.

Santoshi probably expected her brother to kill the king just as Bhima killed Kichaka in defense of Draupadi's honor. What actually happens does not meet with her approval. In her rage, she becomes a malevolent goddess-like being.

In the following story, Krishna not only becomes a woman, he also indulges in sexual intercourse with a man. It is never made clear whether the transformation from Krishna to Mohini is biological (making the intercourse heterosexual) or another case of cross-dressing (making the intercourse homosexual). The story is prevalent only in North Tamil Nadu and is retold in Alf Hiltebeitel's *The Cult of Draupadi*.

KRISHNA BECOMES ARAVAN'S WIFE

The Kauravas and Pandavas fought a great battle on the plains of Kurukshetra. Both were evenly matched. The oracles on the Pandava side divined that human sacrifice was the only way to please the goddess of war and ensure victory. Three men in the Pandava camp were found worthy of sacrifice: Krishna, the divine guide, Arjuna, the commander and Aravan, Arjuna's son by the serpent princess. As Krishna and Arjuna were indispensable, the Pandavas decided to sacrifice Aravan. But Aravan wanted a wife before he was sacrificed, as marriage entitled him to a cremation and proper funerary offerings. No woman was willing to marry a man doomed to die the day after his wedding. So Krishna turned into a beautiful woman called Mohini, married Aravan, spent the night with him, and at dawn, after he had been sacrificed, mourned him as a widow.

In the village of Koovagam, North Tamil Nadu, Aravan is enshrined as Khoothandavar (who is sometimes seen as a parochial manifestation of Shiva). Every year on the full-moon night in the month of Chaitra (February-March), Alis ritually reenact the marriage and widowhood of Krishna/Mohini by becoming the wife of Khoothandavar. The brides call themselves Aravanis. After the sacred thread is tied round their neck, they make love to men who substitute for Aravan. The next day, the idol of Khoothandavar is ritually sacrificed and the Aravanis mourn his passing by breaking bangles, beating their chests, and casting away all bridal finery.[20]

The ritual enactment of widowhood is common in many rites dedicated to village-goddesses or Grama-devis. These rites must be distinguished from sophisticated upper-caste Brahmanical ceremonies dedicated to high-gods such as Shiva and Vishnu. These rustic rites are rather crude and earthy, where the lower castes play significant roles. Sociological studies suggest that since the village-goddess kills her own husband (see Chapter 4), her widowhood is essentially her liberation from patriarchal restraint. It returns to her primal wild state for a temporary period. The period between widowhood and remarriage is marked by orgies (no longer practiced today) and blood sacrifices (prevalent even today) to restore the fertility of the goddess, and hence the village. The unrestrained orgiastic nature of the ritual is believe to be cathartic to the community that comes together once a year during this ceremony.[21]

The sacrifice of Aravan ensures the success of the Pandavas in the great war. After the Pandavas are crowned kings, Krishna returns to his city where he lives like a householder, surrounded by his eight senior wives and 16,100 junior wives. This life lacks the unabashed eroticism of the Maharaas. It is domestic, restrained, and ordinary. Within this ordinary, domestic life occur events that spell the doom of the Yadava clan.

SAMBA'S PREGNANCY

Krishna, lord of the Yadava clan, had a son called Samba, who loved to play pranks. Once, he and his friends decided to have fun at the expense of a few sages who were visiting their city. Samba disguised himself as a pregnant woman and approached them coyly. His friends asked, "Wise sirs, will she bear a son or a daughter?" The sages divined the mischief and were not amused. "Neither," they replied, "He will bear an iron mace that will destroy the Yadava clan." To their horror, a few months later, Samba experienced excruciating pain and delivered an iron mace. When the Yadava elders learned what had happened, they advised the youths to pound the mace and throw the iron powder into the sea. Unfortunately, the powder deposited itself on the beach at Prabhasa and turned into sharp blades of grass. A fish swallowed one sharp scrap of iron that could not be pulverized. The fish was caught by an Outcaste named Jara, a hunter, who turned the iron fragment into an arrowhead. Some time later, the Yadavas went to the beach at Prabhasa for a picnic. They consumed alcohol and began disussing the war at Kurukshetra. Those who sided with the Pandavas began arguing with those who had sided with the Kauravas. Soon the Yadavas were divided into two groups, each one determined to assert their point of view. When words failed, the argument became violent. The men pulled out the blades of grass and began striking each other with them. Unfortunately, these were not ordinary blades of grass. They were as sharp as razors and they struck people dead. Before events could be brought under control, the Yadava men were killing each other. Realizing the futility of trying to stop them, Krishna went to the forest, where he was accidentally struck dead by Jara's arrow.

While Krishna's cross-dressing serves a positive purpose—tricking the enemy, appeasing the lover—Samba's cross-dressing is negative in intention. It seeks to make fun of the sages. The sages are not amused. Instead of exposing the deception, they transform it into reality through the power of their austerities. Samba does become pregnant and does deliver an iron mace that ultimately destroys the Yadava race. Krishna, godhead personified, witnesses the events without raising a finger. He does not stem the march of time. Gods, too, are subject to the law of action and reaction. What is determined by karma must be accepted and endured by all.

When the war at Kurukshetra ended and Krishna stood surrounded by the corpses of fallen warriors, he had to face the wrath of the Kaurava widows. Gandhari, mother of the Kauravas, held Krishna responsible for the death of her sons. In her grief, she cursed Krishna that he too would helplessly witness the death of his children and kinsmen and die a shameful death at the hands of a low-caste man. Karma rules the lives of gods, too. Krishna graciously accepts the reactions to his actions. The price of establishing dharma must be paid.

The story also brings to light that the character of a man is not dependent on his lineage or upbringing. Though Samba is the son of Krishna, he does not display hero-like qualities. In the *Varaha Purana* (c. 750 C.E.), we learn that Samba was cursed with skin disease because he gave in to the amorous attentions of his stepmothers, the junior wives of Krishna.

Samba's behavior and Krishna's death herald the Kali Yuga, the fourth and final age in the life span of the cosmos, when dharma collapses and chaos reigns. According to the scriptures, just as humans die and are reborn, the cosmos also go through cycles of rebirth. Each cosmic life span (known as *Kalpa*) is divided into four ages or *Yugas*. First comes the Yuga known as Krita, at the end of which the "bull of dharma" loses one of its four legs. Then comes the Treta and Dvapara Yuga, when the bull loses his second and third leg. Finally, in the Kali Yuga, lawlessness is rife and the bull loses his final leg and the world disintegrates. A great flood drowns the world, after which the cosmos reemerges purified. In each succeeding age, the life span and height of humans decrease. While in the Krita Yuga, children are produced by thought alone; in the Treta Yuga, they are produced by touch; and in the Dvapara Yuga, they are produced by sex that takes place in the ritually prescribed manner: between man and woman of the same caste bound by marriage during the fertile period. In the Kali Yuga, children are produced through profane (adharma) sex between men and women who do not belong to the same caste and are not necessarily bound by marriage. In the Kali Yuga, men and women have sex even when the womb is not fertile. Men shed semen as base apertures (anus and mouth) of women, and men. They even copulate with animals.[22]

One may conclude that the four Yugas mark a transition from perfection to imperfection and from righteousness to unrighteousness, form order to disorder, the "world of dharma" serving as the standard of all that is perfect, right, and orderly. Implicit in the conclusion is the desire that the retrogressive trend can be reversed. They cannot. Not even the gods can rein in preordained events. Samsara, in many ways, is a self-sustaining entity. Even the gods follow its course.

In every Kalpa, Vishnu descends as Parashurama, Rama, and Krishna toward the end of the Krita, Treta, and Dvapara Yugas. All incarnations have the same mission (upholding order), but each one faces a world with a different measure of dharma. Hence, though the essence remains the same, the identity changes. In each age, as rules of dharma change, so does the social position (determined by caste) of Vishnu's incarnations. He is a priest in the first quarter, a warrior in the second, and a cowherd in the third. In the Krita Yuga, the priest Parshurama obeys his father to the point of beheading his mother (on the grounds that she has had adulterous thoughts) and emasculating his brothers (on the grounds that they refused to kill their mother as their father wanted them to). In the Treta Yuga, the warrior Rama obeys his father, gives his crown to his brother, goes into exile in the forest, remains faithful to his wife, rescues her from the clutches of her abductor, but orders her to leave the palace on the grounds that her reputation has been compromised by her association with her abductor. In Rama's age, sex beyond the confines of marriage and sex with members of the same sex is seen only amongst Rakshasas, described as barbarians and demons. The following episode comes from Makhan Lal Sen's translation of the *Ramayana*.[23]

RAVANA'S HAREM

Hanuman flew into the island kingdom of Lanka in search of Rama's wife Sita, who had been abducted by Ravana, King of the Rakshasas. He entered Ravana's palace and found many women on his bed. Some of them, under the influence of his wife, were kissing the lips of other women, thinking it to be the face of Ravana. The intoxicated women kissed back, believing themselves to be kissed by Ravana. The women were asleep in each other's arms, resting their heads on each other's bosoms, intertwined as garland and spring creeper. Confident that Rama's wife would not surrender her virtue to Ravana, Hanuman left the palace and searched for Sita elsewhere, finally finding her in the royal orchard surrounded by female guards.

The same-sex intercourse here is not a manifestation of same-sex love. It is a poor substitute for cross-sex intercourse resorted to by intoxicated women. The author considers this behavior appropriate for women who are identified as Rakshasas. The Rakshasa women (and men) in the epic are depicted as creatures with insatiable and unbridled sexual appetite, quite unlike Rama and Sita, whose sex lives are regulated by sacred codes. The tendency to dismiss lesbian intercourse as behavior befitting sexually insatiable demons or barbarians is checked by the fact that the Rakshasa-queen Mandodari, wife of Ravana, is considered a holy woman in Hindu hymns. She is described as a "Sati," or chaste wife, worthy of veneration because she remains faithful to her philandering husband and because she stands by him, despite his numerous shortcomings.

Men who, enthralled by Rama's divine aura, desire to be his lover are told to meet him only in the next Yuga. One retelling of this story that is based on the *Ramayana, Padma Purana* (c. 600-750 C.E.), and

Bhagavata Purana, can be found in Wendy Doniger's *Splitting the Difference.*

PAST LIVES OF THE MILKMAIDS

When Rama entered the forest, the sages who saw him, even the trees and animals who looked upon him, wanted to become women and make love to him. Rama, eternally faithful to his wife Sita, rejected their solicitations but promised that when he would incarnate on earth as the cowherd Krishna, they would be born as milkmaids of Vrindavana and dance with him. And so it came to pass. When Krishna played the flute in Madhuvana on moonlit nights, they came as women and dance around him. The cowherds who joined the dance wished they were women too. When Krishna disappeared, the milkmaids in their inability to bear the sorrow of separation, imagined other milkmaids to be Krishna and embraced each other.

What was confined to demons in the Treta Yuga has suddenly made its presence felt in the immediate vicinity of godhead in the Dvapara Yuga. The women in Ravana's bed are other men's wives. The women who dance around Krishna are other men's wives, too. Women in both situations express cross-sex longings in same-sex terms. But the general trend has been to ignore the obvious queerness, strip the stunning imagery of its eroticism and look at the Maharaas as an allegory, insisting that Krishna's love is spiritual *(prema)* not carnal *(kama).* Such interpretations, however justified, cannot take away the encoded bisexuality.

In many *Puranas,* all that is socially unacceptable is considered to be adharma. Their existence is explained as a manifestation of Kali Yuga. As events in Kali Yuga are preordained, nothing can be done about them. With typical Hindu fatalism, therefore, while homosexuality, cross-dressing, intermingling of caste, and liberation of women are condemned, they are also accepted as inevitable events in the march of time.

Vishnu's transformation into Mohini and Krishna's decision to dress as Radha inspire rituals because they support worldly life. These transformations fool or kill demons, villains, and other disruptive forces. They also help appease lovers, reconcile cosmic differences, and unite different theistic schools. But when cross-dressing does not serve dharma, when it opposes gods (Adi), irritates sages (Samba), and angers women (Santoshi's brother), it spells doom and even heralds chaos and anarchy. This is the message driven across through tales where men disguise themselves as women.

Chapter 4

Castrated Men and Women

The practice of appointing eunuchs as servants in harems and women's quarters is believed to have been institutionalized in the land by Central Asian warlords who overran the northern plains of India in the twelfth century of the common era to establish the Delhi Sultanate.[1] But the idea of castration was not unknown in ancient India. In a Jain version of the *Mahabharata,* it is said that when Devavrata took the vow never to beget a child so that his father could marry the ambitious Satyavati (see Chapter 1), he also cut out his genitals, thus ensuring his word could never be broken—even by accident. For this sacrifice, the gods renamed him the awesome one, Bhisma.[2]

The *Mahabharata* records the tale of a eunuch transvestite (kliba) who was appointed as a dance teacher to Princess Uttaraa, daughter of King Virata. This was no ordinary eunuch. This was Arjuna, the Pandava, the most celebrated archer in Hindu lore.

BRIHANALLA: THE EUNUCH DANCER

When the Pandavas lost their kingdom to the Kauravas in a game of dice, they were obliged by the terms of the wager to live in the forest for twelve years and spend the thirteenth year incognito. There was also a clause that should their true identities be discovered during the final year of the exile, they would return to the forest for another twelve years. After enduring the harsh wilderness stoically for twelve years, the five Pandavas hid their weapons, disguised themselves as servants, and sought refuge in the court of King Virata. Arjuna disguised himself as a eunuch transvestite, introduced himself as Brihanalla, the dancer teacher, and gained employment in the royal women's quarters, where he taught dance to the princess, Uttaraa. As the year drew to a close, the Kauravas—whose spies had informed them of the Pandavas' whereabouts—invaded the Virata's kingdom to smoke out their cousins while the king and his soldiers were away chasing cattle thieves. Terrified, the women turned to Virata's young son Uttar, who boasted he would single-handedly drive the invaders away. As there were no charioteers around, Brihanalla offered to take up the reins of the war chariot. This caused great mirth until the prince realized he had no other option. As the two rode toward enemy lines, Uttar caught sight of the formidable formations of the invading army—the shining spears, the array of trumpeting elephants—and panicked. He leapt out of the chariot and ran toward the city. Brihanalla ran after him, caught him by the scruff of his neck, and dragged him back. Those who witnessed this scene roared in laughter. Unable to bear his public humiliation, Uttar decided to end his life, but was stopped by Brihanalla who said he could drive the enemy away provided Uttar served as his charioteer. The prince did not like the idea of serving a eunuch until Brihanalla, after much difficulty, convinced him to have faith. Brihanalla then took the prince to the forest, collected a massive bow from a secret place, strung it, and ordered Uttar to take the chariot straight toward the enemy. There, to Uttar's astonishment, the effeminate eunuch—now transformed into a fierce warrior—shot lethal arrows and in no time drove the invaders away. When the duo returned to the city, Brihanalla resumed his position as charioteer and the palace women—who had not witnessed the scenes in the battlefield— hailed the prince as their savior. Uttar enjoyed the attention for some time, but later confessed the truth. When Brihanalla's true identity was revealed, King Virata was so overcome with gratitude that he offered Arjuna the hand of Princess Uttaraa in marriage. Arjuna politely refused since in his role as dance-teacher he looked upon Uttara as his daughter. Instead, the princess was given in marriage to Arjuna's son Abhimanyu.

Of the five Pandava brothers, only Arjuna changed his gender during the sojourn in hiding. Yudhishtira disguised himself as a Brahmin courtier, Bhima as a cook, Nakula as a groom in the royal stables, and Sahadeva as a cowherd. Their common-wife Draupadi became handmaiden to the queen. Arjuna's choice of disguise has led to (highly controversial) speculations that the author was trying to convey this hero's bisexual leanings.

Speculations are based on several observations and on reading between the lines. Arjuna was the middle brother, third out of five, neither oldest nor youngest (neither here nor there?). His father, Indra, King of the Devas, is described in *Atharva Veda* as "a man amongst men and a woman amongst women"[3] and—as we shall see later in the chapter—is said to be devoid of testicles, but covered with vulvas. He was ambidextrous and could wield his bow with both arms (metaphor for his ability to swing both ways?). He won his wife Draupadi in an archery contest but did not mind sharing her with his brothers upon his mother's request.

To avoid sibling rivalry, the brothers agreed that Draupadi would belong to each one of them exclusively for a year; anyone who entered her bedroom when she was with another brother would be exiled. Arjuna broke the rules, however. He entered her chamber when she was with Yudhishtira (ostensibly to collect his bow) and forfeited his right to her for an extended period of time, during which he was forced to go on a pilgrimage. During this pilgrimage, beautiful women threw themselves at him. He either rejected them or accepted them after much cajoling.

First, there was Uloopi, the serpent princess, who carried him off to her underwater realm. He kept out of her bed until she reminded him that it was against dharma to reject the advances of a willing woman who was in her fertile period. Next, there was Urvashi, the celestial nymph, who he rejected on grounds that she was the wife of his ancestor Pururava and the mistress of his father Indra. Then, he met Chitrangada, Princess of Manipur, whom he loved because she had a manly temperament, according to folk versions of the *Mahabharata*. In Rabindranath Tagore's ballet, "Chitrangada," when she tried to seduce Arjuna by displaying feminine coquettishness, he turned away. She won his love only when she approached him in her true form as a robust warrior maiden. Finally, he abducted and married Subhadra, Krishna's sister, only after Krishna convinced him of the political advantages of such a liaison.

Arjuna was a constant companion of Krishna, much adored by him, and as retold in Chapter 3, the two of them often masqueraded as women to trick their enemies. Before the war at Kurukshetra, when Arjuna displayed hesitation, fear, and doubt, Krishna addressed him as kliba, a non-man, a man who shies away from manly duty, no doubt to prick his male pride and propel him into war. It did not work. It took another sixteen chapters of the divine discourse *Bhagavad Gita* for Arjuna to become "man enough" to pick up the bow and lead his army into battle.

Storytellers and scholars often pass off the year in Virata's court as a comic interlude in an otherwise serious narrative. And it is funny, the idea of a proud swashbuckling warrior, swishing and swirling around unmanned amongst women and children, his battle scars covered with delicate jewelry, his eyes lined with kohl, flashing angry glances at the men who make passes. Even the name Brihanalla translated means "big rod." Brings a smile to the face, doesn't it?

The epic informs us that before employing Brihanalla, Virata had his courtesans confirm his emasculated state. If Arjuna were a virile male who was simply cross-dressing to fulfill an obligation, his deception would have stood exposed. One can argue he did not find the courtesans attractive (he was definitely potent having fathered Shrutakirti on Draupadi, Aravan on Uloopi, and Abhimanyu on Subhadra). Or, maybe he was a castrated male, a eunuch, devoid of manhood. This was a temporary state, lasting for a year, according to the following story, which incidentally does not form part of the classical edition and is believed to be a later-day interpolation.[4] The episode can be found in Kesari Mohan Ganguly's translation of the *Mahabharata* and has been dramatized in Peter Brook's film *Mahabharata*.

URVASHI CASTRATES ARJUNA

Arjuna, son of the King of the Devas, Indra, once paid a visit to the heavenly city of Amravati where he was taught dancing by the gandharvas. During his stay, Urvashi, the fairest nymph of all, fell in love with him. Bedecked in celestial splendor, Urvashi approached Arjuna and sought his embrace. He refused to indulge her. "You are the beloved of my father Indra and were once wife to my ancestor Pururava. Embracing you would be nothing short of incest," he explained. "I am a nymph," said Urvashi, "I belong to no one. I can go to whomever I please. The morality of mortals does not apply to me. Come, let us make love." Arjuna refused because mortal rules still applied to him. Peeved by his intransigence, Urvashi hissed out a curse, "Only a eunuch refuses a willing woman. So be one," and walked away in a huff. When Indra heard of the curse, he told his son, "Curses cannot be revoked, but they can be modified. You will lose your manhood, as Urvashi wills it, but only for a year of your choice." So it came to pass. Arjuna was obliged to spend one year of his life without his manhood.

Arjuna turned the curse to his advantage in the thirteenth year of his exile when he became Brihanalla. It is interesting to note that despite confirming Brihanalla's emasculated state a year earlier, when Virata was informed of the eunuch dancer's true identity, he feared that his daughter's reputation may be compromised by her year-long association with a "man." He immediately gifted Uttaraa away to Arjuna. Arjuna accepted the princess not as his wife, but as his daughter-in-law.

In the *Brahmavaivarta Purana* (750 to 1550 C.E.), the enchantress Mohini says, "A man who refuses to make love to a woman who is tortured by desire is a eunuch." When a willing fertile woman approached a man, he was obligated by dharma to have intercourse with her. Bound by sacred law, sages (such as Vaishrava) were sometimes even forced to satisfy demonic women (such as Kaikeshi). Such unions resulted in the birth of powerful villains (such as the Rakshasa-King Ravana) and there was nothing the gods or sages could do to stop it.

Men who refused to lay with women during their fertile period, for whatever reason, were cursed and doomed, since they were denying an ancestor a chance to be reborn. In the following folk story from the state of Gujarat, castration is the punishment for a man who denies his wife her right over his manhood. It was told to me by a devotee of Bahucharji-mata, whom I met in Ahmedabad, a city not far from the shrine of the goddess. Another version of this narrative can also be found in Serena Nanda's book *Neither Man nor Woman: The Hijras of India*.

BAHUCHARA EMASCULATES HER HUSBAND

Bahuchara's husband never came to her at night. Instead he would mount his white stallion and ride out into the forest. Determined to unravel this mystery, one night Bahuchara decided to follow him. But she had no horse. A giant jungle fowl, witness to her plight, offered himself as her mount. Bahuchara mounted the fowl, scoured through the forest, and finally found her husband in a clearing behaving like a woman. "If you were like this, why did you marry me and ruin my life?" asked Bahuchara. Her husband explained that he was forced into marriage so that he could father children and continue the family name. Feeling cheated, yet sorry for her husband, Bahuchara declared, "Men like you should castrate themselves, dress as women, and worship me as a goddess."

It is never made clear what exactly Bahuchara witnesses in the forest. In some versions, she finds her husband naked and suspects that he is having an extramarital affair. It turns out that he was drying his clothes after taking a bath in a river. The goddess castrates him by mistake and suffers (as all over-suspecting wives are supposed to) as a result. No explanations are offered as to why he wants to have a bath in a river at night when his beautiful bride waits for him in his palace. In another retelling, he is said to behave "like a Hijra." What does this mean? Does it mean he was being effeminate? Does it mean he was wearing women's clothes? Does it mean he was having sex with men? The truth is only implied, never stated. In yet another retelling, when she wrenches off her husband's manhood she cries, "I have taken what I need from you. You have no use of it," indicating that for a wife, a husband's value lies primarily in his ability to beget children on her. It also suggests that she may have witnessed her husband as a passive homosexual. This is, of course, pure speculation since oral tales are difficult to substantiate.

Popular calendar art of the goddess show her riding a jungle fowl. Hijras castrate themselves in the name of this goddess. The castration is described as nirvana (Buddhist word for liberation). The ritual unites the Hijra with the goddess, transforms him into a Bhagat (a devotee). The practice of castration in the name of the goddess is reminiscent of self-castrating priests of the ancient Anatolian goddess Cybele, who sought to emulate the self-castration of her beloved Attis who had incurred the goddess's wrath when he succumbed to the affections of the hermaphrodite/eunuch Agdistis.[5]

It is believed that the goddess Bahuchara visits men whom she wants to be her Bhagats in their dreams. She torments them until they agree to shed all symbols of masculinity, including their manhood. Infertile women, in their quest for fertility, often invite Bhagats to sing songs to the glory of the goddess so as to invoke her grace. They serve as servants, mediums, or priests of the goddess. One wonders if the "call of the goddess" is a call to homosexual/transsexual men not to marry and ruin lives of women. Bahuchara's rage perhaps expresses the frustration of women who are tricked into such unions, an extremely common occurrence in India even today. Bound by tradition to adjust and submit, the frustration of women trapped in similar situations often explodes into "hysterical fits," described in folk Hinduism to be "the arrival of the goddess." Since a woman's suffering is viewed as necessary for social stability, involuntary seizures resulting from repression are celebrated as the mark of the divine. When a woman gets her convulsions, villagers gather around to greet the goddess and salute her medium.

Castration is a recurrent theme in stories associated with Bahucharji-mata. In the following tale retold in Pupul Jayakar's book *The Earth Mother,* the goddess castrates not only her assailant but also herself in order to save her honor.

BAHUCHARA CUTS HER BREASTS

Bahuchara and her two sisters were on their way to a fair when a marauder called Bapiya attacked their caravan. To escape rape and abduction, the sisters killed themselves. Bahuchara cut her breasts. As she bled to death, she cursed Bapiya that he would become impotent. When Bapiya begged for mercy, Bahuchara said he would be forgiven only if he wore women's clothes and worshipped her as a goddess.

The curse of impotency is, in effect, an act of castration. Both Bahucharaji-mata's undersexed husband and oversexed assailant suffer loss of manhood. Both men "become women" and are asked to worship the woman they abuse. Castration is thus punishment of the extremes. It is the fate of the homosexual man and the heterosexual rapist. In between lies dharma, righteousness, and balanced conduct.

The story of Bahuchara introduces the concept of female castration, where breasts are substituted for testicles. Breasts are the visible erotic protrusions that define a woman's sexuality, just as the penis defines a man's sexuality. By removing her breasts, Bahuchara makes herself "unworthy" of violation. She becomes a non-woman and destroys that which her assailant seeks to violate. In doing so, she destroys herself.

In both stories, Bahuchara's procreative powers are not realized. Untapped, the creative energy becomes destructive and spells doom for those responsible for her suffering. The theme of sexual frustration, female castration, and destructive energy resonates in the story of Kannagi found in the Tamil epic *Silappadikaram* (c. 500 to 600 C.E.), retold by Lakshmi Holmstrom.

KANNAGI PLUCKS OUT HER BREAST

Kannagi's husband the merchant Kovalan spent all his wealth on the courtesan Madhavi. Kannagi suffered silently. When all the money was gone and with it Madhavi's affections, Kovalan returned to his chaste wife. The couple decided to move to the city of Madurai and start life afresh. At Madurai, Kannagi gave Kovalan one of her gold anklets studded with diamonds to raise capital. The goldsmiths accused Kovalan of stealing the queen's anklets and had him killed before he could present his case. When Kannagi learned what had transpired, she strode into the king's court, the other anklet in hand, demanding justice. When the king realized he was at fault, he begged Kannagi to forgive him. But Kannagi was too angry to forgive. She plucked out one of her breasts and hurled it into the city square, where it burst into flames. Soon the whole city was on fire. Nearly everyone was burned to death. Those who survived turned Kannagi into the goddess Pattini, enshrined her image, and appeased her wrath.

Both Bahuchara and Kannagi are apotheosized following their refusal to be victims. The anguish, frustration, outrage, and indignation—resulting from a man's wrongdoing—turns them into "hot" goddesses who can be appeased only with blood sacrifice, blood of a male animal symbolizing semen in keeping with the traditional medical belief that a thousand drops of blood make one drop of semen. Both Bahuchara and Kannagi transform into what are known as Grama-devis, village-goddesses believed to be parochial manifestations of the supreme mother-goddess Mahadevi.[6]

As mentioned in Chapter 1, nearly every Indian village has a Grama-devi shrine and each shrine is associated with the tale of a woman who has suffered violence or injustice at the hands of a man. The stories of Bahuchara and Kannagi are variants of the common theme of a woman who discovers that her husband is no Brahmin, but an Outcaste. Such is her rage at being duped that she kills her husband and burns down her house, herself and her children with it. She rises out of the flames as a terrifying goddess, whom the villagers appease with sacrifices of male buffaloes, goats, and fowls. A man who claims to be something he is not has also betrayed Bahuchara. In her case, the issue at hand is sexuality, not caste. While the former situation results in castration, the latter is rectified by death.

In the following story, unutilized creative energy of a god becomes destructive. The story is based on narratives from the *Mahabharata, Shiva Purana, Varaha Purana,* and *Linga Purana* (c. 600 to 1000 C.E.). It establishes Shiva as Sthanu, lord of the fiery phallic symbol. Various versions of the story have been retold in Wendy Doniger O'Flaherty's book *Shiva: The Erotic Ascetic.*

SHIVA CASTRATES HIMSELF

Brahma asked Shiva to create the world. To do so, Shiva hid in the waters and began to meditate. Eons passed. When he did not emerge, Vishnu asked Brahma to create the world and populate the world with various creatures. Eventually Shiva rose from the waters. When he saw the world was already created he was furious. He opened his mouth and spat out fire. Brahma begged him to stop. Shiva controlled his rage and wondered, "What is the use of my seed since creation has already been achieved?" He tore out his manhood and hurled it into the air. It transformed into a pillar of fire, rising above the skies, and descending below the foundations of earth. Brahma took the form of a swan but failed to find its top. Vishnu took the form of a boar, burrowed deep into the earth, but failed to find its base. Acknowledging Shiva's supremacy, Brahma and Vishnu worshipped his magnificent symbol—the fiery pillar.

The self-castration of Shiva is not as much a part of popular lore as is the appearance as his fiery phallic symbol, the *jyotir-linga.* As explained in Chapters 1 and 2, retained seed is so full of energy that it makes the penis dazzle with power. Unused for creation, Shiva's manhood reverberates magnificently with divine energy, overwhelming the gods. In some *Puranas,* Shiva emerges from this pillar itself to bless Brahma and Vishnu. In others, the divine manhood is restored to its rightful place on Shiva's body. In still others, it calms down when the mother-goddess contains its power in her womb.

Shiva is often described as ithyphallic, in a state of constant arousal. Images of the ithyphallic god meditating or dancing adorn many temple walls. But Shiva's arousal has no cause. There is no urge to spill the seed. No desire to react, respond. The arousal has no reason, purpose, or result. It is pure. Pure arousal, pure bliss—*ananda*—the eternal emotion of the blessed.

In the following story from the *Shiva Purana,* sages mistake Shiva's arousal to be an expression of lust for their wives. Enraged, they castrate Shiva. The story has been retold in Wendy Doniger O'Flaherty's *Shiva: The Erotic Ascetic* and in Sadashiv Ambadas Dange's *Encyclopaedia of Puranic Beliefs and Practices,* Volume IV.

SAGES CASTRATE SHIVA

Naked with penis erect, Shiva wandered into a forest in a state of inebriation, oblivious of his surroundings. In the forest lived sages whose wives were so besotted by his body that they chased him like mad women, begging him to embrace them. The sages blamed him for arousing adulterous thoughts in their wives and cursed him to lose his penis. Instantly, Shiva's manhood dropped to the ground. It transformed into a fiery missile and threatened to destroy the whole world. Terrified, the sages invoked the mother-goddess, who took pity on them and caught the fiery missile in her womb and contained its destructive power.

Here, sexual rivalry provokes castration. The sages attack and emasculate the man they suspect to be their wives' paramour. When the power of Shiva's semen born of asceticism reveals itself, the sages realize their folly. Shiva, the ascetic, has no attachment. He is no rival, though others may perceive him as one, and feels nothing about being deprived of his manhood. In one version, when the sages hurl accusations at Shiva and demand that he be castrated, he castrates himself without remorse or resentment. Shiva is said to be inebriated on hemp when he enters the forest, blissfully unaware of his surroundings, unaware of prejudices and insecurities that permeate human habitation. When the sages castrate him, they are unable to bear the fiery consequence and are forced to call open the mother-goddess. Only the water in her womb can transform the destructive fire into a creative force.

In the *Naradasmriti,* a medieval law text, castration is the punishment for a variety of sexual offences, including having sex with mother, aunt, mother-in-law, sister, and nun.[7] In the *Ramayana,* castration is viewed as a just punishment for adultery. It is applied to both men (Indra) and women (Surpanakha).

INDRA LOSES HIS MANHOOD

Indra took the form of a rooster and began to crow hours before daybreak, giving the sage Gautama the impression that it was dawn already and time for his morning ablutions. When the sage stepped out, Indra entered the hermitage disguised as the sage and asked the sage's wife Ahalya to have sex with him. Though surprised at this untimely request, Ahalya—the dutiful spouse—complied. Gautama, meanwhile, saw the moon, realized it was still night, and returned to the hermitage, only to find his wife Ahalya in the arms of Indra. In his fury, he cursed Ahalya to turn into a stone, to be stepped on by all creatures. He then castrated Indra. The Devas got together and managed to restore Indra's manhood. Gautama also cursed Indra that his body would be covered with a thousand vulvas. Years later when chaste Rama came to the hermitage of Gautama, he found the stone that was once Ahalya. Such was the purity of his being that when he stepped on the stone, he liberated the sage's wife from the curse.

The virility and manhood of Indra, King of the Devas, are the objects of hyperbolic praise in the *Rig Veda.* He is a rain-god, a fertility god, and a god with the roving eye, always on the lookout for women left unattended by their husbands. In the *Mahabharata,* Indra's actions arouse discomfort but are never condemned. To protect his wife from the amorous attentions of this virile god, one sage Devashrama orders his student Vipula to use his magic powers, enter his wife's body, and restrain her from within.[8]

In the *Ramayana,* with its more rigid codes of morality, Indra's actions are tolerated as long as they function within the parameters of social law. When Indra tricks Ahalya, a married woman, into having sex with him, he crosses the line and faces a terrible consequence. As an epic, the *Ramayana* is all about restraint, obedience, and upholding the law at any cost for the sake of social order. It does not even spare the unwitting victims of sexual acts, such as Ahalya and the epic's heroine, Sita. The former is turned to stone, the latter is rejected by the hero Rama on grounds that her long sojourn with her abductor Ravana has compromised her reputation and made her unworthy of being his queen.

Sex, in the *Ramayana,* is acceptable only when marital law regulates it. The epic contrasts the monogamous and ever-faithful hero, Rama, to the villain, the rakish Ravana, molester of women. It also contrasts Sita, the chaste wife of Rama, to Surpanakha, the sexually unrestrained sister of Ravana. The story of Surpanakha's mutilation is found in most retellings of the *Ramayana,* with minor variations. In some, only the nose and ears are cut; in others even the breasts are not spared.

LAXMANA MUTILATES SURPANAKHA

> Palace intrigues forced Rama to a fourteen-year exile into the forest. His dutiful wife Sita and brother Laxmana followed him there. In the final year of their exile, the trio camped on the banks of the river Godavari. When Surpanakha, the widowed sister of the King Ravana, saw Rama she was overwhelmed by desire. Rama, however, rejected her solicitations on grounds of marital fidelity. Determined to have Rama, Surpanakha decided to kill Sita and take her place. As she rushed toward the startled Sita, Laxmana blocked her path. He raised his sword and hacked her nose, her ears, and some say, even her breasts. Surpanakha complained to her brother who decided to avenge her humiliation by abducting Rama's wife Sita, and forcing her to be his queen.

In traditional Hindu society, a widow does not remarry. She is supposed to remain faithful to their husband's memory. The widow Surpanakha's lustful behavior confirms her identify as a barbarian, a Rakshasa (see Chapter 1). In the "Uttara Ramayana," the last chapter of the epic, we are informed that Ravana, in his quest to be overlord of the Rakshasas, had accidentally killed his brother-in-law. To make amends, he had given his sister rights to all the men she found in the forest. Unfortunately, one of the men she liked turned out to be Rama, lord of civilized behavior, under whose supervision the unbridled sexuality of Surpanakha was reined, through symbolic castration. Male castration involves the cutting of penetrative power; female castration involves destruction of feminine charm (indicated by nose, ears, and breasts). While female castration saves a woman's honor in Bahuchara's tale, it brings shame in the story of Surpanakha.

Male castration can result when manliness, rather than manhood, is brought into question. The following story has no scriptural basis. It is a popular folk tale from the district of Belgaum in Karnataka. It forms the foundation of a much-disgraced religious tradition of dedicating boys and girls to Renuka-Yellamma, the goddess who resides on the boundaries between the field and the wilderness, between chastity and wantonness.

EMASCULATION OF JAMADAGNI'S SONS

Renuka was roused by the sight of a king making love to his queens on the banks of a river. When her husband, the sage Jamadagni, divined the adulterous thoughts in her heart, he was furious. He ordered his sons to behead their unchaste mother. His five elder sons refused. Only the youngest, Parashurama, raised his axe to behead his mother. She ran to the village of Outcastes in the hope her son, a high-caste Brahamin, would not follow him for fear of ritual pollution. But Parashurama, determined to carry out his father's orders, followed her there. One woman called Yellamma tried to come before mother and son to prevent the crime of matricide. The resolute Parashurama swung his axe and ended up beheading both the woman and his mother. Then, instructed by his father, he emasculated his brothers. Later, pleased with Parashurama's unquestioning obedience, Jamadagni offered his son a boon. Parashurama asked that his brothers and mother be revived. In his hurry to rejoin his mother's head and body, Parashurama exchanged the heads so that two women came into being—one with a Brahmin head and Outcaste body, another with an Outcaste head and a Brahmin body. Who was the mother of Brahmins? Who was the mother of Outcastes?

All around the village of Saundhatti in Belgaum, even in the red-light districts of cities like Mumbai and Pune, women can be seen carrying pots or wicker baskets. On the rim is attached a metal head

of the goddess Renuka-Yellamma. The goddess is smeared with vermilion and turmeric powders and adorned with bridal finery, peacock
feathers, and cowries. These women are called devadasis, servants of
the goddess, or jogatis, holy women given to her in marriage. The
women are her priestesses. They never marry. They go from house to
house singing the praise of the goddess and accepting alms on her behalf for their subsistence. Similar to the goddess with a transposed
head, who belongs neither to Brahmins nor to Outcastes, but is a bit
of both, these women are neither married nor unmarried. They belong
to no single man and hence are available to all. They are similar to the
goddess, everyone's woman/mother (in Kannada, ella = everyone; in
Kannada, amma = mother). They are viewed as sacred harlots,
women for the taking. The devadasis of Belgaum have no source of
income and more often than not earn a living by prostituting themselves. They are raised to believe that offering their bodies to anyone
who desires it is their sacred duty, to the outrage of social reformers.

Among the women are men known as jogappas (jogi = yogi = holy
man; appa = father in Kannada), who wear female apparel, carry the
effigy of the goddess on their head, and live their lives as women.
These men are believed to be doubles of Parashurama's brothers who
were not men enough to carry out their father's orders. In some versions, the brothers are beheaded. In others, they are emasculated.
Symbolic not biologic castration, social denial of manhood, is the
price of disobeying the dharma of man. Around their necks are beads
that bind them to the boundary goddess. In keeping with tradition,
they also offer their bodies to men who seek pleasure.[9]

The practice of dedicating women more than men to gods was
fairly common in medieval times. Temples had devadasis who served
as sex workers and added to the income of the temple.[10] In most temples that employed devadasis, the presiding deity was male. For example, in Puri the women were dedicated to Jaggannath, a form of
Vishnu-Krishna. Yellamma is an exception where women are dedicated to goddess. Some experts believe that the devadasis of Yellamma
are not attendants of the goddess, but instead are her diminutive doubles, who are deprived of marital status and social standing just as the
goddess is. Others are of the opinion that she is dedicated to her son
Parashurama (thus taking away any homoerotic suggestions between
the women and the goddess), and appointed by him to serve as priestesses of Yellamma.

In the following story of Chelliamman, a woman is clearly dedicated to a goddess to serve as a substitute for a husband that she has been deprived of. The same-sex, divine-mortal union is viewed in ritual, not carnal terms. The story was told to me by C. S. Lakshmi, who heard it from Shri Annamalai (Imayam).

CHELLIAMMAN'S FEMALE COMPANION

> When the gods and demons churned the ocean of milk for the treasures dissolved in it, there emerged many magnificent treasures. Some treasures—animals, plants, gems, weapons—they divided amongst themselves. Others, like nymphs, they agreed to share. Then the waters spewed forth poison, from which came Mudevi, the goddess of sloth and sleep. No one wanted to marry her. Then from the waters came the elixir of immortality, from which rose Sridevi, who was the goddess of fortune. Sridevi decided to become the wife of Vishnu, who had another wife, Bhudevi, the earth-goddess. Then came two more women: Chelliamman and Tara. Chelliamman was given in marriage the two brothers, Sugriva and Vali, the rulers of Kishikinda, the land of monkeys. "I will not marry two men," said Chelliamman. "I don't mind," said Tara. So Tara became the common-wife of Sugriva and Vali. This left Chelliamman. She refused to be single as Mudevi was, she refused to be a co-wife and share a husband as Sridevi was, and she refused to be a common-wife and be shared by many men as Tara was. "Who shall take care of me?" she asked Shiva, the wise hermit-god. Shiva decreed that humans would dedicate a woman to be her companion and attendant. This companion would remain a virgin, and their union would be ritually celebrated each year in a grand ceremony.

The story forms the basis of a practice in a village in the southern state of Tamil Nadu, of dedicating a woman to serve the goddess. She is bound by tradition to stay away from men and take care of Chelliamman. Unlike other women and men dedicated to gods and goddesses (known as devadasis), the women dedicated to Chelliamman are not sexually exploited, but they do face extreme social and economic hardships due to their ritual status. This traditional practice has met with severe criticism because it deprives the woman of her basic rights and reduces her to abject poverty.

The question may be asked, "If Chelliamman needed an attendant, why were men not dedicated to her?" The explanation could lie in the traditional belief that men who touch the village-goddess become impotent or die at an earlier age, as the goddess saps their virility. Hence, in many parts of India men who approach fiery village-goddesses do so dressed in female apparel.

Tradition prevents Chelliamman's female attendant from tapping her fertility. This is highly unusual in Hinduism, where fertility is given prime importance in the ritual scheme of things. Fertility forms the foundation of samsara. The cycle of fertility involving sex, birth, nourishment, disease, and death is the cycle of the goddess, the cycle of Nature. Compared to Buddhism and Jainism, monastic ideals are given lesser importance in Hinduism. Sex may be regulated by dharma, chastity may be promoted as a virtue, but celibacy is acceptable only *after* biological obligations have been kept. A man can renounce the world and be a sanyasi only after he has lived the life of a householder or *grihasthi*.

Men who did not shed their seed in the womb were viewed with suspicion. They either shed semen in what the law books described as base wombs (mouth or anus of men, women, and animals) or they retained semen to gain spiritual prowess (see Chapter 1). The former were ostracized or castrated. The latter were seduced.

Sages who would not marry and who, if married, avoided intercourse, were deemed to be too self-absorbed to be concerned with the welfare of the Pitrs (see Chapter 1). Their refusal to be generative, their stepping away from the orderly sequence of generations, from between the past (forefathers), and future (offspring), was seen as a direct attack on samsara. And samsara struck back, tormenting them with visions of suffering ancestors.

In the *Mahabharata*, in a dream the sage Jaratkaru sees his forefathers hanging upside down like bats over the pit of oblivion. Realizing he was the cause of their suffering, he vows to marry, father children, assist in their rebirth, and return to the forest only after repaying his debt.[11] In the *Bhagavata Purana*, Devahuti shows her husband Kardama the way to pay his debt to his ancestors without compromising his spiritual purity. "Make love to me without passion during the fertile period and you will father a child without losing your chastity," she said. Once the child is born, Devahuti lets her husband go. He has completed his biological obligations and is needed no more.[12]

In the following story, the sterility resulting from a man who stays away from women has an adverse impact on Nature. Even though Hindu lore leans toward spiritual reality, ascetic pursuits are unacceptable if they harm material reality. The story from the *Mahabharata* is retold in Benjamin Walker's *Hindu World,* Volume II, while Wendy Doniger O'Flaherty's essay "Androgynes" in her book *Sexual Metaphors and Animal Symbols in Indian Mythology,* recounts the Buddhist retelling of the same.

THE MAN WHO HAD NEVER SEEN A WOMAN

The sage Vibhandaka remained continent in his quest for spiritual knowledge. One day, the sight of a nymph bathing in a river caused him to spill semen. A doe grazing nearby ate the semen and in due course delivered a male child called Rishyashringa. Vibhandaka raised Rishyashringa without any knowledge of womanhood. Rishyashringa grew up without ever seeing a woman. He became a great ascetic. So intense was his austerity that it irked Indra, the rain-god, who refused to let the clouds shed rain until someone overpowered Rishyashringa and forced him to give up his asceticism. The resulting drought forced the hand of King Lompada who sent his daughter Shanta and an entourage of courtesans to seduce the young sage. When the young ascetic Rishyashringa saw Shanta, he felt a strange stirring in his loins. "Who is this man," he wondered, "with peculiar but delightful things on his chest." He questioned "him" about his lack of manhood. Shanta replied, "It was lost in an accident. Please relieve the pain." Rishyashringa helped the wounded "man" and ended up making love to Shanta. No sooner had he shed his semen than Indra let the rain fall and the drought was over.

In Buddhist lore, when Rishyashringa (Isisinga) tells his father about this (female) man, the father, instead of enlightening the son, says, "That was a Yakshini," frightening the boy into returning to his austerities. In the *Mahabharata,* this is how the young man describes the man in the forest: "He was a chaste youth, with long hair and perfumed body. He had two globes beneath his neck, which he said greatly oppressed him and at his suggestion I stroked and kissed them to relieve his distress. He had a narrow waist and rounded hips. He took me by the hair and set his mouth on mine and brought my soul to a shuddering delight. And when he pressed his body to mine my senses seemed as they would leave me. He had a small mollusk-like mouth in the public region, which he explained was torn by an arrow, and at his suggestion, I soothed him as he required. Now that he has gone my body burns within me." Describing the "man" as a "demon," Vibhandaka sets out in search of the wily intruder. While he is away, Shanta returns and coaxes the willing Rishyashringa to come with him to her father's kingdom. Vibhandaka follows his son there determined to curse the abductors. However, when the king explains his desperation, the sage permits Rishyashringa to stay with the woman, but only until he had fathered a child. Then, after his obligation to the cycle of rebirths has been fulfilled and another ancestor was reborn, Rishyashringa would return to the spiritual realm.

The story of Rishyashringa is extremely homoerotic because here the ascetic makes love to a "man" who happens to have a female body. Through Shanta's eyes, the intercourse is heterosexual. Through Rishyashringa's eyes, it is intercourse with a man—a man who is not quite a man, a man with delightful things on his chest, a man with a scar between his legs. The story ultimately reconciles the twin aims of worldly life—procreation and liberation. We are left to wonder if the author was commenting on the dangers of arousing same-sex longings in men deprived of women.

In Hindu lore, the threat of castration harnesses fertility to social order. A man who does not behave as a man (Parashurama's brothers), a man who does not go to his wife (Bahuchara's husband), and a man who rejects a willing fertile woman (Arjuna), are castrated. Castration is also the fate of men (Indra, Bapiya, and Shiva) and women (Surpanakha) who do not respect the chastity of women or the sanctity of marriage. Overutilization or underutilization of procreative powers threatens stability. Between the two lies the civilized society, where the unrestrained sexuality of Nature and the sterility of spirit are reconciled.

Chapter 5

Neither This nor That

Often, the truth is neither this nor that. Or rather, it is a bit of both—this *and* that. The truth can rest on the threshold, in the twilight, somewhere in the middle, between contradictions, slipping in as a possibility between two realities. This possibility is a recurring theme in Hindu lore, the best example for which is the story of Narasimha, the man-lion incarnation of the god Vishnu, found in the *Bhagavata Purana* and retold in Kamala Subramaniam's *Srimad Bhagavatam*. Vishnu, the guardian of cosmic order, rests on the waters of possibility, hence is also known as Narayana.

NARASIMHA

The Asura Hiranakashipu had obtained a boon that made him near immortal: he could be killed neither by a man nor a beast, neither by a weapon nor a tool, neither inside a house nor outside, neither at day nor at night. Thus empowered, he attacked the Devas and took control of their celestial city, Amravati. Hiranakashipu declared himself to be the lord of the world and threatened to kill anyone who dared worship anyone but him. To his great surprise and annoyance, his son Prahalad, who was enlightened in the ways the supreme divine principle, spent every waking moment of his life chanting the divine name of Vishnu: "Narayana, Narayana." Hiranakashipu did everything in his power to scare or distract his son into silence. He failed miserably. Finally, he asked Prahalad, "Where is this Narayana? Show him to me and I shall kill him. That will put an end to your obsession." Prahalad replied, "He exists everywhere. Even in the pillars of your palace." To prove him wrong, Hiranakashipu smashed a pillar with his mace. Out came a fantastic creature that was neither man nor lion, who grabbed the

Asura with his claws, which is neither a weapon nor a tool. It dragged Hiranakashipu to the threshold, which is neither inside nor outside a dwelling, and at twilight, which is neither day nor night, ripped open his belly, wrenched out his heart and squeezed out his life. This monster was Narasimha, the man-lion, a manifestation of Vishnu-Narayana.

Possibilities beyond human imagination always exist. The manifestation of such possibilities displays the limitations of the human mind and helps one appreciate the divine.

Possibility is expressed in Hindu lore through liminal beings such as *Kimpurushas* and *Kimnaras* (Kim = what?; purusha = nara = men/beings; "queer" creatures?), who, similar to *Devas* (celestial beings), Asuras (cthonian beings), *Apsaras* (water nymphs), *Gandharvas* (divine musicians), *Nagas* (serpent beings), Rakshasas (barbarians), *Yakshas* (goblins), *Vidyadharas* (keepers of occult lore), and *Manavas* (humans), are progeny of *Brahma,* the creator. Incidentally, the Hijra community in some parts of North India call themselves Kinnara.

In art, possibility is expressed through images of fantastic beings, chimeras and dragons, and animals who exist at the interface of two species, such as the bird-headed lion shardula, the elephant-headed cat yali, the elephant-headed fish makara, and the eight-legged, three-horned dragon sharabha. On temple walls, the entire spectrum of real and imagined cosmic activity is magnificently displayed: monks meditate next to dancing nymphs, warriors fight while lovers copulate, musicians and dancers perform as gods bless, demons terrify, trees blossom, and animals hunt. Things that are otherwise hidden adorn sacred gateways or the sanctum sanctorum: men making love to horses, orgies involving harlots and sages. The inexplicable, the unimaginable, are displayed nonchalantly to the alarm of the visitor: tigers playing with deer, elephants mating with lions, gods drinking blood from human skulls, goddesses feeding on corpses, demons meditating. Even godhead manifests simultaneously in two contrasting forms—a world-affirming cosmic king (Vishnu) and a world-rejecting cosmic ascetic (Shiva).

In the *Mahabharata,* before the war at Kurukshetra, when Krishna displays his cosmic form, Arjuna shrinks back in terror and begs the lord to return to his human form.[1] Within the cosmic form Arjuna saw all possibilities, all realities, all world views. Before such a vision, every certainty is reduced to insignificance. Man is jolted out of the complacent belief that he can comprehend the cosmos. He is humbled into appreciating every manifestation of the divine.

In the Vaishnava tradition, Narasimha is a manifestation of the "neither this, neither that" cosmic possibility. For the *Shaivas*, this idea is brought home in the form of Ganesha, the elephant-headed son of Shiva's consort, Parvati (Gauri).

Ganesha is also called Vinayaka (vina = without; nayaka = male protagonist), because no man participated in his birth.[2] Unlike viras such as Hanuman, Ayyappa, and Kartikeya, he is all female, born without contribution from the male seed, but still ayonija, nonwomb born. The following story of Ganesha's birth is found in the *Shiva Purana* and retold in Paul Martin-Dubost's book *Ganesha: Enchanter of the Three Worlds* and in the Amar Chitra Katha comic book *Ganesha*.

CREATION OF GANESHA

Whenever Parvati asked for a child, her consort Shiva would say, "We are immortals. Why do we need progeny?" But Parvati, surrounded by Shiva's servants known as Ganas, was lonely. She wanted a child who would love and obey only her. She wanted a child who, unlike the Ganas, would prevent Shiva from entering her abode when she sought privacy. Determined to have such a child, she scrubbed off the sandal-turmeric paste she had anointed herself with, molded a doll out of it, and breathed life into it. Parvati declared the child thus born to be her son. She named him Vinayaka and ordered him to guard the door of her cave and not let anyone in. The boy stopped everyone, even Shiva, from entering his mother's cave. In his fury, Shiva raised his trident and beheaded the boy. Parvati was inconsolable with her grief. She threatened to destroy the world with her fury. To placate his wife, Shiva decided to revive the boy by placing on his headless body the head of the first creature who passed his way. That creature turned out to be an elephant. So it came to pass that Parvati's child ended up with the head of an elephant and the body of a man. Shiva declared him Ganesha, Lord of all Ganas. He became the guardian of thresholds, he who keeps the undesirables out. Everyone adored him as the remover of obstacles and the lord of beginnings.

In Randolph and colleagues' *Cassel's Encylopedia of Queer Myth, Symbol, and Spirit,* based on observations made by P. B. Courtright in his book *Ganesha: Lord of Obstacles, Lord of Beginnings,* we are informed that Malini, Parvati's handmaiden, helped the goddess create the child. The story (originally from Jayadratha's *Haricharitachintamani*) is that the elephant-headed Malini drank Parvati's bathwater and delivered a baby with five elephant heads. Shiva cut four of the five heads and accepted the child as his own.[3] The same book informs us that Shiva replaced Vinayaka's head with that of a cow elephant. These retellings lend a homoerotic twist to the conception of Ganesha. He becomes a horizontally androgynous deity—female head, male body—created by two women.

These points, of two women creating Ganesha or of the elephant head being female, do not figure either in popular retellings of the narrative, as in mythological films such as *Hara Hara Mahadeva,* television serials such as *Om Namah Shivaya,* the comic book series Amar Chitra Katha, or in scholastic works such as Shakunthala Jagannathan and Nanditha Krishna's *Ganesha: The Auspicious... the Beginning* and Paul Martin-Dubost's *Ganesha: Enchanter of the Three Worlds.* One wonders if this is a case of deliberate "queering" of a narrative?

The idea of two women giving birth to a child is less acceptable in Hindu lore as compared to the idea of two men (Shiva and Vishnu) giving birth to a child. The discomfort makes itself known in the following story from the *Padma Purana* and the Bengali *Ramayana* by Krittivasa (c. 1400 C.E.), which has been retold in Giti Thadani's *Sakhiyani,* in Wendy Doniger's *Splitting the Difference,* and in the book *Same-Sex Love in India,* edited by Ruth Vanita and Saleem Kidwai.

TWO QUEENS CONCEIVE A CHILD

King Dilip had two wives but no children. So he requested sages to generate a magic potion that would make his wives pregnant. Unfortunately, he died before the potion could be put to use. Not wanting to waste the magic fluid, the two widows came up with a plan. One queen drank the potion and the other made love to her in the manner of a man. The plan worked. The queen became pregnant, but nine months later she delivered only a lump of flesh. This the sages attributed to the absence of men in the rite of conception. The sages then used their powers to rectify the mistake.

In this story same-sex intercourse serves as a poor substitute to cross-sex intercourse and predictably, the results are disastrous. Since, according to the scriptures, a child's bones and consciousness come from the male seed, while blood, entrails, and flesh come from the female seed,[4] the child born is devoid of bones or consciousness. It is just a ball of flesh, which the sages have to revive through the power gained by austerities.

There are those who may argue that the role of Malini has been deliberately ignored, downplayed, or appropriated to fit the patriarchal and heterosexual discourse. This is a frequent issue in Hindu lore. With so many variants, why is one retelling given more importance over the others? Why is the story of Ganesha receiving his elephant head from his father more important than the variant from the *Uttar Ramayana,* retold in Vettam Mani's *Puranic Encyclopaedia,* where Ganesha's elephant head is the result of Shiva and Parvati making love taking the form of elephants?

The elephant killed to revive Vinayaka is unlikely to have been female because in Hindu rituals, sacrifice of female animals is expressly forbidden. It brings bad luck. Whenever a blood sacrifice is offered to fierce deities such as Kali or Durga, the animal slaughtered is always male, be it a buffalo, ram, or rooster. In the *Brahmavaivarta Purana,* it is clearly stated that the gods beheaded Airavata, the celestial white-skinned bull elephant who rose from the ocean of milk (see Chapter 3) and served as the mount of Indra, King of the Devas.

From a Freudian viewpoint, Ganesha's androgyny is inferred from his broken tusk (suggesting emasculation), his trunk (limp and unthreatening in contrast to Shiva's erect and throbbing manhood), his "breast-like" temples, and his plump unmuscled body indicative of water (hence feminine) personality in Ayurveda. The fact that he is his mother's child, that he never leaves his mother's side, that he prevents his father from forcing an entry into his mother's abode, that he is beheaded by daring to do so, all suggest—to a Freudian—mother fixation, sexual rivalry with the father, an inability to relate to women sexually, and a rather simplistic Oedipal analogy.[5]

Such interpretations seem to align themselves with the a Tamil folk tale that explains Ganesha's single status. The story is recounted by A. K. Ramanujan in his essay "The Indian Oedipus" compiled by Vinay Dharwadker.

GANESHA REMAINS SINGLE

Once Parvati asked Ganesha who he would like to marry. Ganesha replied: "Someone exactly like you, Mother." Angered by this openly incestuous wish, the goddess cursed her son with everlasting celibacy; that is why he is still a bachelor.

Correlating Ganesha's infantile fantasy to his celibacy would horrify a Tamil devotee, for whom Ganesha's chastity, or brahmacharya, fits in perfectly with his role as the celestial scholar and scribe, to be invoked before commencing any activity. The tale itself is not popular or preserved in any popular or revered scripture. In their opinion, to equate celibacy with "lack of interest in women," is perhaps taking interpretive liberties a bit too far.

Ganesha is not a bachelor in all traditions. As with his brother Kartikeya, Ganesha's marital status is ambiguous. In northern India, Kartikeya is a bachelor, while in southern India traditions he has two wives. The roles are reversed in the case of Ganesha. While Kartikeya does not marry because "all women are his mother," Ganesha does not marry because "no woman is as good as his mother." In both cases, bachelorhood stems from mother fixation.

In Bengal, Ganesha is said to have married the banana plant in desperation because no other woman wanted to marry an elephant-headed god. The banana plant, known as Kola Bou, is also the symbol of Ganesha's mother Gauri. Thus the identity of mother and wife are blurred. Likewise, in Bengal, incestuous links are suggested between Kartikeya and his mother, Durga, in folktales that inform us that when peacocks noisily trespassed and found the goddess in a compromising position with her son, they were cursed with impotence and an ugly squeal. Later, the goddess allowed them to have offspring by means of tears.[6]

In Tantra art, Ganesha is often shown embracing his shakti using his so-called "flaccid" trunk rather erotically. In this tradition, he is the guardian of the Muladhara chakra, the first gateway to the occult mysteries that governs animal instincts and is located at the base of spine between the anus and the scrotum. In occult biology, seven gateways are located in the body, strung by the spine like a garland. At the base, coiled up, is the Kundalini—potential energy—waiting to be roused through the base chakra. Through various rituals involving chants *(mantra)*, visualization *(tantra)*, and sacred diagrams *(yantra)*, Ganapati is invoked and the Muladhara gateway opened so the Kundalini can rise like a serpent and pierce through five other gateways before stimulating the flowering of the final chakra on top of the head, giving the aspirant access to the secrets of the cosmos.[7]

The *Shiva Purana* states that Ganesha has two consorts known as Siddhi and Buddhi (Siddhi and Riddhi or Riddhi and Buddhi in other traditions). Siddhi means accomplishment, Riddhi means prosperity, and Buddhi means intellect. The *Purana* also states that the two wives of Ganapati have borne him two sons: Kshema (prosperity) and Labha (profit). According to one folk story, which inspired the popular Hindi film *Jai Santoshi Maa* (1975), Ganesha even has a daughter, Santoshi, goddess of satisfaction. The wives and children of Ganesha may be seen as embodiments of all things that arrive when Ganesha is invoked. This, along with his corpulent form suggestive of prosperity; his elephant head suggestive of strength and power; his mount, the rat, suggestive of unstoppability, makes Ganesha, the celibate bachelor of the south, a fertility god of the north.

Ganesha clearly stands between the male (spiritual) and female (material) realms. At first he prevents the penetration of Shiva into the realm of Gauri. Later, he reconciles the conflict by becoming the son of Shiva, taking on the name Ganesha, Lord of Shiva's hosts. In his celibate form, he satisfies monastic aspirations of knowledge and transcendent power. As a householder, he satisfies mundane worldly aspirations of wealth and prosperity. In his Tantrik role as guardian of the Muladhara chakra he resides between the penis (symbol of penetrative power, activity, and masculinity) and the anus (symbol of receptive power, passivity, and femininity). He removes all obstacles, enabling one to move with ease from one construct to another, from one paradigm to another, from one world view to another.

A mind-set, which adores half-human, half-animal beings such as Narasimha or Ganesha as manifestations of the divine, does not find it difficult to make room for the idea that out there in the world exists creatures who are neither male nor female. One of the earliest expressions of this possibility can be found in the following story from the *Jaiminiya* and *Tandya Brahmanas* (c. 800 B.C.E.), ritual texts based on the *Vedas*. Wendy Doniger O'Flaherty retells the story in her book *Sexual Metaphors and Animal Symbols in Indian Mythology*.

THE SEPARATION OF THE THREE WORLDS

> At first the three worlds were united. Then the gods separated them. With separation came sorrow. The gods removed this sorrow and put it elsewhere. The sorrow of earth was put into the whore, the sorrow of the heaven was put into the rogue, while the sorrow of the atmosphere was put into the eunuch.

In the previous story, earth is visualized as feminine, heaven as masculine, and atmosphere as neuter. Their respective sorrows go to the oversexed female, the rule-breaking male, and to one who is neither male nor female. This being who is neuter is not just a mythical entity, but a biological possibility, according to the *Mahabharata*. The epic states that a child is conceived in the womb when the red seed of woman merges with the white seed of man. If the white seed is powerful, male children are conceived; when the red seed is powerful, female children are conceived; when both seeds are equally matched, a hermaphrodite is conceived.[8] Hermaphrodite here may mean many things: someone having both male and female biology (genetic or hormonal hermaphrodite); someone with a male biology but female personality or female biology but male personality (transsexual, transvestite, homosexual); or someone with both male and female personalities (bisexual).

Traditionally, when a man fathers only female children, he is considered a weak man whose seed is less potent than that of his wife. In Ayurveda, a prescription of herbs, breath control, and exercise is prescribed to make the body strong and semen potent so that only male children are conceived. Despite such attempts to create a world populated only with men and women who comfortably fit into the patriarchal and heterosexual construct, there was always a conscious attempt to acknowledge and make room for those who did not fit in the straight and narrow. In the Jain tradition, for example, there are three types of sexual cravings that can ensnare the soul in the flesh: desire for men, desire for women, and deire for hermaphrodites.[9] Likewise, those who do not fit in the binary heterosexual framework of society created spaces for themselves by appropriating mainstream ideas. This comes across in the following story from the oral tradition of the Hijras that has been recounted in Serena Nanda's *Neither Man nor Woman: The Hijras of India* and in Wendy Doniger's *Splitting the Difference.*

RAMA'S RETURN

King Dasharatha decided to crown his eldest son Rama King and retire into the forest for a life of contemplation. However, on the eve of the coronation, his junior wife Kaikeyi summoned him to her quarters and demanded the two boons he had promised her years ago, on the day she had saved his life on the battle-field. "Let my son Bharata be crowned king instead and let Rama live in the forest as a hermit for fourteen years." Bound by his word, Dasharatha ordered Rama into exile. When the residents of Ayodhya heard of the happenings in the palace, they were heartbroken. They decided to follow Rama into exile, for they loved him so. When Rama reached the river that separated his father's kingdom from the forest, he turned around and said, "Men and women of Ayodhya, if you truly love me, wipe your tears and return to my brother's kingdom. I have to go into the jungle alone. We shall meet again in fourteen years." The men and women of Ayodhya obeyed Rama and returned to the city. But those people who were neither men nor women did not know what to do. They could neither follow Rama nor return to Ayodhya. They remained on the banks of the river until Rama returned. Rama blessed them and decreed they would be kings in the age of darkness, Kali Yuga.

When this story was narrated on a television talk show, many in the audience dismissed the tale on grounds that it does not form part of the "original" *Ramayana.* As explained in Chapter 2, there is no "original" *Ramayana.* Since its earliest recorded retelling in Sanskrit nearly 2,000 years ago, there have been several hundred *Ramayanas,* in several languages, some put down in writing, others existing only in oral form, each satisfying the needs of a particular period or a people. In *Jain Ramayanas,* for example, Rama upholds the Jain value of nonviolence and leaves the killing of the villain to his brother

Laxmana.[10] The *Ramayana* in the *Devi Bhagwatam* (a scripture dedicated to the mother-goddess), focuses on female power and chastity. The Ramayana of the Hijras does not deviate from the grand subtext: the supreme importance of unquestioning obedience for the sake of social order. By remaining true to the spirit of the epic, the retelling empowers the Hijra community. Rama, divine upholder of social laws, not only acknowledges their existence, but also grants them a boon to make up for his earlier oversight. Today, Rama is more than just a symbol of augustness, fortitude, and righteousness, worthy of reverence and worship. He has been appropriated by the Hindu right wing and transformed into a powerful political icon. The Hijra retelling, with its prophetic overtones, has the potential of generating outrage and controversy, since it grants power to a people who are considered by traditionalists as threats the social order and the dominant discourse.

One of the most common images used to represent one who is neither man or woman is the Ardhanareshwara, the half *(ardha)* woman *(nari)* god *(eshwar)*. What does this image mean? Does it mean the divine is both male and female? Does it mean all creatures contain maleness and femaleness within them? Does the image evoke gender equality? Is a symbol of self-containment, fulfillment, wholeness?

To answer these questions, we must understand the evolution of this image. The concept of a divine androgyny originated from the *Upanishads*. The *Upanishads* mark the speculative phase of Hinduism between Vedic ritualism (1500 B.C.E. to 500 B.C.E.) and Puranic theism (500 C.E. to 1500 C.E.). During this phase, scholars and seers sought to decipher the mysteries of life, the first of which was: How did the world come into being? The following story comes from the *Brihadarayanaka Upanishad*. It has been retold in R. C. Zaehner's *Hindu Scriptures*.

PURUSHA SPLITS INTO TWO

In the beginning there was only the soul in the likeness of a man. Looking around, he saw nothing other than himself. First of all he said: "This is I." Thus I-ness came into the world. He realized he was all alone. With that realization came fear and loneliness. To be rid of these feelings, he decided to create another. He split himself into two and created another, the second, the woman.

He united with her and the world came into being. She thought, "He who has generated me now copulates with me." Not appreciating this, she turned into a cow; he became a bull. He copulated with her, thus cattle were born. She became a mare; he became a stallion. She became a ewe; he became a ram. She became a goose; he became a gander. She became a doe; he became a buck. Thus, all creatures came into being.

Primal unity, howsoever self-contained, needs to be shattered if the world has to manifest itself. Equilibrium lacks creative tension. Self-containment is sterile. Only when there are two can there be love and hate, sex and violence. Only when there are two can the cycle of life rotate. In the *Upanishad,* two ideas are interlinked. Since the spirit is clearly identified with man, the woman must be matter. Thus, the gender split is also a splitting of metaphysical principles.

The idea of splitting is further elaborated in the *Puranas,* where the abstract idea of Purusha is personified as Brahma, the creator. Here, initial creation without intercourse is found inadequate. A helpless Brahma is inspired by a vision of androgyny to split in two. Only when the male half copulates with the female half do all sorts of creatures populate the universe. The following story is based on retellings from various *Puranas.* They are retold in Wendy Doniger O'Flaherty's *Shiva: The Erotic Ascetic.*

BRAHMA SEES THE HALF-WOMAN GOD

In the beginning, the primal lotus bloomed and out came Brahma. He was all alone so he decided to create another. From his thoughts he created sons. These mind-born sons refused to procreate. Brahma was in a fix. He frowned and from the frown rose Shiva, in the form of an androgyne. His left half was the goddess Shakti, his right half was he himself. The two halves split: from the right half came males, the left half came females. Brahma ordered the males and females to have intercourse and reproduce.

The previous narratives make it very clear that cosmic dynamism happens only after two principles emerge from the primal oneness. Copies of Brahma, his mind-born sons, are sterile. Fertility emerges only when the androgyne splits. In some versions of the narrative, it is

Brahma who splits in two (as the Purusha of the *Upanishad*) and he
copulates with his female half. This act, viewed as incestuous, arouses
cosmic disgust. Shiva expresses his outrage by wrenching off one of
Brahma's five heads. Thus Shiva, who inspires the split of the androgyne, also opposes the split. Shiva, the destroyer, destroys the primal
stillness. He also seeks to destroy the division of male and female,
spirit and matter, and return to primal unity. Shiva splits and fuses.
The split is procreative. The union is sterile. Shiva thus oscillates between splitting and fusing, fertility and sterility, eroticism and asceticism.

As in the *Upanishad,* the splitting of the Puranic androgyne does
not clarify if the split is metaphysical or biological. Are the two
halves abstract principles, such as spirit and matter? Or are they biological concepts, such as maleness and femaleness? Or is one to pre-
sume that Shiva is male, hence spirit, and Shakti is female, hence
matter?

At this point it makes sense to tackle the common error of equating
Chinese (Taoist) principles of yang and yin, activity and passivity, hot
and cold, male and female, with Hindu concepts of Shiva and Shakti,
purusha and prakriti, brahman and maya. Though opposites of each
other, Shiva/Purusha/brahman is *not* yang while Shakti/prakriti/maya
is *not* yin.

Shakti/prakriti/maya represents energy, Nature, delusion, everything that transforms, that can be perceived by the senses, con-
structed within by space and time, contained by name and form. By
contrast, Shiva/purusha/brahman is spirit, soul, self, truth, everything that is beyond transformation, beyond definition, beyond
space and time, beyond name and form.[11] The eighth-century philosopher Shankara described the latter through negation, *neti-neti,* not
this-not that. The former then is the rest, *iti-iti,* this too-that too.

The best translation for yin and yang in Tantra is *ida* and *pingla,*
the cold and hot, lunar and solar, the left and right, the female and
male aspects of material things. Between the two lies *shushumna,* the
balanced state, the tao.

The pingla flows on the right side of the body since it is male. The
ida, the female energy, flows on the left. In all Ardhanareshwara images, the right half is invariably male and the left half female. The left
side has always been used to denote womanhood in Hindu art. A wife

always sits to the left of the husband. In the following folklore, the goddess Parvati fuses with Shiva to assert her position as his consort.

SHIVA MAKES PARVATI HIS LEFT HALF

The sage Bhagiratha invoked the gods and begged them to let the celestial river Ganga flow on earth to help the living wash away their sins and to help the dead make a smooth transition to the next life. The river-goddess Ganga agreed to descend but warned the sage rather pompously, "The earth will not be able to withstand the force of my fall." So Bhagiratha invoked Shiva and requested him to break Ganga's fall by trapping her in his mighty locks. Shiva agreed and stood on the highest peak on earth, ready to receive the descending river-goddess. The haughty Ganga soon found herself entangled in Shiva's hair, her gush reduced to a trickle. When Shiva's consort Parvati saw the river-goddess Ganga caught in her husband's hair, she was not amused. "You call me your wife but let another woman sit on your head." To placate Parvati, Shiva embraced her until she merged and became the left half of his body.

There are many reasons given for association of the left half with womanhood. With the woman on the left, the man's right hand is free to wield the sword or hold the scriptures. The left side of the body is controlled by the right brain (seat of the traditionally female trait of intuition). The heart is located on the left side of the body. Thus, the wife sits on the side that is closer to the heart. According to the following folklore, the Ardhanareshwara form is an expression of Shiva's love for Parvati.

SHIVA FUSES WITH PARVATI

Shiva, the hermit, never brought food home for the family. He just meditated, danced, or smoked hemp. Tired of managing the household on her own, Parvati left the house with her two sons, Kartikeya and Ganesha. Shiva did not miss them until one day he experienced hunger. He went in search of food but found none. He even begged for food but failed to obtain any alms. Desperate, he went to the Devas who advised him to go to the city of Kashi where a woman served food to whosoever came to her door. Shiva went to this woman and she placed a bowlful of rice before him. After eating his fill, Shiva looked up and realized that the woman feeding him was none other than Parvati. Realizing her value, he embraced her with so much passion that they fused into one body.

A wife is known as *vamangi* (angi = body). *Vama* means both woman and the left. It also means the antinomian, the heretical, the inauspicious. Gifts are never given or received with the left hand, food is never touched with the left hand, blessings are never conveyed through the left hand because the left hand is ritually impure, used only to perform ablutions. Thus, a gender inequality is implicit in the image of Ardhanareshwara. Woman and matter, though necessary, occupy inferior positions.

The left-handed path, or *Vamachara* (achara = behavior), is the antinomian path of spiritual growth based on Tantrik ideas, while the right-handed path, or *Dakshinachara,* is the mainstream path of spiritual growth based on Vedic ideas. In the former, the material world, hence woman, is shakti—the source of all power—to be invoked, celebrated, and realized through all five senses. In the latter, the material world, hence woman, is maya—delusion due to ignorance—whose seductive powers can overwhelm the mind and who needs to be restrained through dharma or sublimated through yoga. In the former, women play a central role; truth lies in them. In the latter, women play a supportive role; truth lies beyond them. In the former, no distinction is made between the sacred and the profane, the impure and the pure; thus Tantrik rituals include carnal, anthropophagic, and scatophilic practices. In the latter, strict rules of pollution and ritual purity govern all aspects of life. The former indulges flesh, intuition, and spontaneity. The latter is governed by intellect and restraint.

Shiva is the lord of Vamachara. His shakti is so close to him that she has been internalized and transformed into his left half. Even when Shiva does not display his female half, he projects his androgyny by wearing women's earrings in his left ear. This reflects both the union of as well as freedom from opposites. Shiva, the destroyer, thus destroys division. He destroys the fettering binary paradigm. He unites, he liberates. That which makes him the object of admiration also makes him the object of ridicule. Hence the words used to praise him in the *Shiva Purana:* "You are not a god or a demon or a mortal or an animal; you are neither man, woman or eunuch," are no different from the words used to revile him in the *Skanda Purana:* "He has no caste and is neither male nor female. He cannot be a non-male because his phallus is an object of worship."[12]

The man who reviles Shiva the most is the priest-king Daksha, a son of Brahma, Lord of Dakshinacha. In the *Puranas,* he is presented as the patron of yagna, the ritual that forms the foundation of traditional Vedic society. A keeper of orthodox dharma values, he gave wives to all the gods. Much to his vexation, his youngest daughter, Sati, chose to marry Shiva. For Daksha, Shiva represented the force of chaos and destruction, one who preferred breaking rules and transcending constructs. This was reaffirmed when, though his son-in-law, Shiva refused to salute him.

Contemptuous of everything Shiva stood for, Daksha came up with a plan to put Shiva in place. He conducted a grand sacrifice and invited all gods to partake the oblations. All except Shiva. Unable to bear this elaborate insult meted out to her husband, Sati walked into her father's sacrificial chamber and leapt into the sacred fire to her death. With the altar contaminated with Sati's blood, the yagna ground to a halt. When Shiva learned of his consort's death he lost his temper. Transforming into Bhairava, the fearsome one, he unleashed his fury into the cosmos. Unrestrained, Shiva raised his sword, beheaded Daksha, picked up Sati's corpse, and danced like a madman in grief, threatening to destroy the world with his unbridled sorrow. To protect the world from untimely dissolution, Vishnu cut Sati's corpse into tiny pieces. With the corpse gone, Shiva's anger dissipated and he retired into a cave. He shut his eyes, restrained his senses, transcended all anger and desire, and refused to step into the world outside, once again threatening cosmic stability—this time with sterility—until Parvati (Sati reborn as the princess of the mountains) came along and, after many austerities, won a place in his lonesome heart. He embraced her so forcefully that they became one.[13]

In the following story from Karnataka retold by A. K. Ramanujan in his essay "On Folk Mythologies and Folk Puranas," compiled by Vinay Dharwadker, Shiva becomes half a woman because of a curse. This is a folk story and unlike its classical (Sanskrit, Brahmanical) counterpart, here splitting and creation stems from the will of the mother-goddess Adishakti.

SHIVA CURSED TO BECOME AN ANDROGYNE

Adishakti came into being three days before the three worlds came into being, three days before Brahma, Vishnu, and Shiva were born. She attained puberty and with it came desire. She first created Brahma, but he refused to satisfy her passion as she was his mother. Enraged, Adishakti burnt him to ashes. Next came Vishnu. He too turned down her request. Enraged, Adishakti burnt him too. Then came Shiva. He tricked the goddess into giving him her third eye and all her powers before he was willing to satisfy her. Shiva then burnt Adishakti to ashes instead. Before she turned into a heap of ash, Adishakti cursed Shiva, "Since you rejected me, a woman like me will get stuck to you and become half your body." Later, Shiva revived Brahma and Vishnu. They divided the ash mound into three and out of them came the goddesses Saraswati, Laxmi, and Parvati, who married Brahma, Vishnu, and Shiva, who took them to their abodes in Brahmaloka, Vaikuntha, and Kailas.

Metaphorically, the Ardhanareshwara image reconciles two conflicting ideas: male and female, spirit and matter. The following story retold by Wendy Doniger O'Flaherty in her essay "Androgynes" in the book *Sexual Metaphors and Animal Symbols in Indian Mythology,* shows the dangers of not acknowledging one half of the divine pair.

BHRUNGI TRIES TO SEPARATE THE ANDROGYNE

To express his devotion, Bhrungi wanted to go around Shiva. Parvati stopped him. "Shiva and I are a pair. You cannot worship him in his totality without acknowledging me. Hence you must go around both of us" But Bhrungi wanted to circumambulate only Shiva, not Parvati. To make this impossible, Parvati sat on Shiva's left lap. Bhrungi tried squeezing between them to have his way. So Parvati fused her body with Shiva's and became his left half. Determined not to include Parvati in his worship, Bhrungi turned into a bee and tried to bore a path between the left and right halves of Shiva's body. Peeved at his insolence, Parvati cursed Bhrigu that he would lose that part of his body that emerges from the female seed. Immediately, Bhrugni lost all flesh and blood and collapsed on the ground. Reduced to nothing but bones, Bhrungi apologized and sang songs to the glory of the goddess. Finally, the god and the goddess showed mercy and gave him a third leg to enable him to stand upright. He still had a skeletal frame to remind him of the importance of the goddess.

The story of Bhrungi's loss of muscle mass is based on the belief that half the body's constituents come from the female seed. Just as a child cannot be conceived without both man and woman, truth cannot be realized without acknowledging both spirit and matter. This is the point the goddess drives into Bhrungi.

Uniting two complementary concepts in one body is a common artistic tool employed in Hinduism. The image of one being—half male, half female—unites two complementary concepts: maleness and femaleness, spirit and matter. Sometimes, the two halves are male, as in the case of Hari-Hara, a composite image whose left half is Vishnu and right half is Shiva, or vice versa. If the Ardhanareshwara image is seen in biological or psychological terms as the union of maleness and femaleness, of the outer and inner self, what does the union of two male gods symbolize? In the Hari-Hara image, two complementary (or antagonistic) ideas come together—world affirmation and world negation, householder values and ascetic ideals. Vishnu represents the former, Shiva, the latter.

In the Vaishnava tradition, Vishnu forms the right half of the Hari-Hara image. This suggests that the right half (the male half) is the dominant position. The identity of the androgyne is derived from the right side. Ardhanareshwara, despite being half female, is considered male, a manifestation of Shiva, not Parvati. She is *his* half. He is not hers. Along similar lines, it is significant to note that the *linga,* Shiva's phallic symbol, is his symbol, not hers. This, despite her forming the foundation.

SHIVA-LINGA

Once, while Shiva and Parvati were making love in a cave, sages sought an audience with them. They called out, but Shiva was so entranced that he did not hear them. When Shiva did not reply, the sages entered the cave and found the divine couple locked in embrace. Embarrassed, Parvati covered her face with a lotus. Shiva, in a state of mystical passion, did not even notice the sages and continued making love to his consort. Disgusted, the sages decreed that Shiva would be worshipped forever without form, as a pillar in a trough, symbolizing his manhood in the womb of the goddess, the divine lingam in the divine yoni.

The pillar-like linga stands in a basin—identified with the womb of the goddess Parvati—that points to the left. Above is a perforated pot—identified with Shiva's second consort Ganga—that drips water on the linga. Thus, the linga is located between Parvati below and Ganga on top. The devotee rarely sees the consorts. All attention is directed at the linga. The basin and the pot, symbols of earth and fertility, are summarily ignored.

As Hinduism moved from ancient Vedic ritualism to medieval Puranic theism, spiritual reality came to be viewed as superior to material reality. Material reality became merely the medium through which the spirit expresses itself and the means through which the spirit could be realized. A Krishna may want to make love to himself and create Radha out of his reflection,[14] but ultimately he will leave her when duty beckons (see Chapter 3). Implicit in concepts such as detachment and sublimation, so inherent in Vaishnava and Shaiva philosophy, is the feeling that matter (and by extension woman) is the lesser though necessary half of the divine. Ultimately, though their approaches may be contrasting, both the Dakshninachari and the Vamachari, the householder and the ascetic, have a common goal—dominate women and gain power over material reality.

Ardhanareshwara has great appeal both for analytical psychologists as well as psychoanalysts. The Jungian would look upon it as a symbol uniting the "persona" and the "soul image" (animus/anima, depending on which gender's viewpoint one is coming from) so that the "shadow" can be overpowered and the "self" realized. The idea that every man has a woman inside forms the foundation of the following folklore compiled by A. K. Ramanujan and retold by Wendy Doniger in her book *Splitting the Difference.*

THE PRINCE WHO MARRIED HIS LEFT HALF

A prince did not want to marry but when his parents insisted that he take a wife, he cut his body in two; the right half healed to become a full man, the prince, while the left half became a woman whom the prince married. The prince kept his wife in a deserted place and rarely visited her. A wizard fell in love with the prince's wife and became her lover, visiting her in the form of a snake. The king caught and killed the snake as it was slipping into the palace through a hole in the wall. In grief, the woman refused to eat. She gave a mendicant one coin for finding the dead snake, two coins for cremating it, and three coins for putting the ashes in a talisman that she tied round her neck. As the days passed, the woman became thinner and unhappier. She simply clung to the talisman round her neck. The prince asked her the reason for the sorrow. "How can I be happy when you have imprisoned me and rarely bother to visit me?" The prince offered to visit her every day. "No, instead hear my riddle. If you answer it, I will kill myself. If you don't, you will kill yourself." The riddle was: "One for seeing, two for burning, three for wearing round the neck; a lover on the shoulder, a husband on the thigh." The prince heard the riddle but could not answer it. So he killed himself and his left half, the wife, took another lover and lived happily.

The story is full of fodder for Freudian psychoanalysis. It captures the conflict between the superego (the king), the ego (the prince), and the id (the woman who makes up his left half). While the prince acknowledges the existence of the woman inside him through marriage, he represses her by refusing to satisfy her sexually. She demands satisfaction and makes her feeling known through adultery. The king, however, does not appreciate this and destroys her paramour. The tension mounts and finally there is a confrontation between the two halves of the prince, the man and the woman, the ego and the id. Who shall survive? The answer to the riddle is a truth that the man wants to repress: his left half's erotic desires. The woman inside him wants to satisfy her lust with a man. Rather than answer the riddle, the man kills himself. The ego succumbs before the needs of id. All the superego can do is watch as primal instincts take over. The woman inside the prince gets her way. She gets the man.

Maybe there is a man and woman in all of us. Who shall we satisfy? Who is our true self? Is it the sex imposed upon us by biology, the gender imposed upon us by society, the desire that lurks in the mind or the sexless, genderless, desireless spirit within us that is waiting to be discovered? The discovery shall be made, say the Hindu scriptures, as we give meaning to our lives *(purushartha)* through the balanced fulfillment of social obligations (dharma), economic wants (artha), erotic cravings (kama), and spiritual needs (moksha). Since there is no one approach to life, the individual trapped between instinct and intellect, private longings and public duties, has to make his or her choice of obligations, wants, cravings, and needs. In those choices, or beyond them, he or she will discover who he or she really is. In realization lies release. And release is the ultimate goal of all existence.

In the Hindu world, possibilities stretch beyond the imagination. Thus, there is no certain truth. Narasimha is neither man nor animal. Ganesha is both man and animal. Shiva is neither the austere hermit nor the amorous householder. Vishnu is both the straightforward Rama as well as the wily Krishna. Man is not totally male; there is a woman inside him. Woman is not totally female; there is a man inside her. So where does identity come from? Where does validation come from? From within or from without, from desire or from duty, from biology or psychology, from the left half or the right, from the stillness of the spirit or from the throbbing sensuousness of the body. As we make our choices, cling to our timorous world views, grapple with our ephemeral constructs, we will find our answer. But the final answer, the ultimate absolute truth, will be neither this nor that.

Afterword

The Hindu worldview considers every behavior and identity a possibility in this endless, boundless, cyclical universe. Hindu society, however, with its foundations in patriarchy and heterosexuality, deems nonconventional gender identities and sexual behaviors inappropriate for social stability. They are tolerated only in fringes, especially if they express themselves through patriarchal and heterosexual vocabulary. This conflict between Nature and culture, and the resulting repression of choices that threaten the dominant discourse, is manifest in the queer plots and queer characters of Hindu lore.

Queer tales, though subversive from one point of view, are conformist from another because they endorse traditional gender roles and sexual symbolism. In narratives where men become women and women become men, feminine imagery continues to represent material reality, while male biology provides the wherewithal for spiritual prowess. Thus, throbbing beyond sexual politics, time-honored metaphysical metaphors and allegories retain their mythic power.

Hindu lore also drives home the point that social law changes with time to meet the demands of a particular age. What is dharma in the age of Rama need not be dharma in the age of Krishna. The world changes with time and with it human behavior and social law. Modern Indian law is often at odds with Hindu belief, ritual, art, and narratives, making no room for alternate sexual behaviors and gender identities, despite their existence in traditional constructs, probably because it borrows heavily from British colonial law that was largely formulated within the Judeo-Christian scheme of things. The presumption that what is "unnatural" in the biblical paradigm must be "unnatural" within the Hindu paradigm disregards the fact that Hindu lore projects everything as part of Nature and of divinity, governed by the law of karma. Some things may be socially inappropriate. But nothing is unnatural. In fact, everything is a manifestation of the divine.

Notes

Introduction

1. Graves, Robert. *The Greek Myths*. London: Penguin Books, 1960.
2. Randolph, P., Lundschen, Conner, Hatfield Sparks, David, and Sparks, Mariya. Agditis, Attis. In *Cassell's Encyclopedia of Queer Myth, Symbol, and Spirit*. London: Cassel, 1997, pp. 39-40.
3. *The Greek Myths*.
4. Spencer, Colin. *Homosexuality: A History*. London: Fourth Estate, 1995, pp. 47-51.
5. Durgadas, Ganapati Sivananda. Confessions of a Tantric Androgyne. Published in the Web site <www.anythingthatmoves.com>.
6. Flood, Gavin. *An Introduction to Hinduism*. New Delhi, India: Cambridge University Press, 1998, p. 1.
7. Translation circulated in Web pages by the Association Against Religious Vilification and World Vaishnava Association following the outcry against the "Homosutra" Mardi Gars in Sydney, 1999, where Hindu imagery was used rather irreverently.
8. Nabar, V. and Tumkur, S., trs. Chapter 7. In *Bhagavad Gita*. Hertfordshire, England: Wordsworth Classics, 1997, p. 29.
9. Doniger, Wendy and Smith, Brian K. *The Laws of Manu*. New Delhi, India: Penguin Books, 1991, p. 58.
10. Ibid., p. 257.
11. Translation circulated in Web pages by the Association Against Religious Vilification and World Vaishnava Association following the outcry against the "Homosutra" Mardi Gars in Sydney, 1999, where Hindu imagery was used rather irreverently.
12. Panati, Charles. *Sexy Origins and Intimate Things*. New York: Penguin Books, 1998, p. 493.
13. Mentioned in Muraleedharan, T. The Writing on Absent (Stone) Walls. *Thamyris*, Spring 1998.
14. *The Laws of Manu*, p. 191.
15. Donaldson, Stephen. Prison Sexuality: Prisons, Jails, and Reformatories. In Dynes, Wayne R., ed., *Encyclopedia of Homosexuality*. New York: Garland Public, 1990.

16. These lines are my own. They appear at the start of all of my books, expressing my belief that the sacred narratives, symbols, and rituals we are exposed to since childhood create our worldviews.

Chapter 1

1. Jaini, Padmanabh S. *Mahabharata* Motifs in the *Jaina Pandava Purana*. In *Collected Papers on Jaina Studies*. New Delhi, India: Motilal Banarsidass Publishers Pvt. Ltd., 2000, p. 355.

2. Ramanujan, A.K. The Indian Oedipus. In Dharwadker, Vinay, ed. *The Collected Essays of A.K. Ramanujan*. New Delhi, India: Oxford University Press, 1999, pp. 377-397.

3. *Collected Papers on Jaina Studies*, p. 355.

4. Kinsley, David. Village Goddesses. In *Hindu Goddesses: Visions of the Divine Feminine in the Hindu Religious Tradition*. New Delhi, India: Motilal Banarsidass Publishers Pvt. Ltd., 1987, pp. 197-208.

5. Sebastian, K.C. Same-Sex (Female) Lovers Commit Suicide. In *Sameeksha* [Malayalam fortnightly], June 28 to July 11, 1998.

6. Sebastian, K.C. Lesbian Suicides Continue. In *Sameeksha* [Malayalam fortnightly], June 1-15, 1999.

7. Posters of twin goddesses, such as Chamunda and Chotila, are commonly sold on the streets of Mumbai. One print is found in Pattanaik, Devdutt. Companions of Devi. In *Devi, the Mother Goddess—An Introduction*. Mumbai, India: Vakil, Feffer and Simons, 2000, p. 79.

8. Doniger, Wendy. *Splitting the Difference*. New Delhi, India: Oxford University Press, 2000, p. 247.

9. Devi, Shankuntala. *The World of Homosexuals*. New Delhi, India: Bell Books, 1978, pp. 145-147.

10. *Bhagavad-Ajjuka Prahasanam* (The Farce of the Saint-Courtesan), quoted in *Splitting the Difference*, p. 296.

11. *Collected Papers on Jaina Studies*, p. 387.

12. Ibid., pp. 391-394.

Chapter 2

1. Meyer, Johann Jakob. *Sexual Life in Ancient India*. New Delhi, India: Motilal Banarsidass Pub. Pvt. Ltd., 1989, p. 498.

2. Quoted in O'Flaherty, Wendy Doniger. *Sexual Metaphors and Animal Symbols in Indian Mythology*. New Delhi, India: Motilal Banarsidass Publishers Pvt. Ltd., 1981, p. 308.

3. O'Flaherty, Wendy Doniger, tr. *Rig Veda: An Anthology*. New Delhi, India: Penguin Books, 1994, pp. 182-185.

4. Ramanujan, A.K. Three Hundred Ramayanas: Five Examples and Three Thoughts on Translation. In Dharwadker, Vinay, ed. *The Collected Essays of A.K. Ramanujan*. New Delhi, India: Oxford University Press, 1999, pp. 144-146.

5. Richman, Paula, ed. *Many Ramayanas: The Diversity of Narrative Traditions in South Asia*. Berkeley and Los Angeles: University of California Press, 1991.

6. Frawley, David. *From the River of Heaven*. New Delhi, India: Motilal Banarsidass Pub. Pvt. Ltd., 1992, pp. 115-118.

7. Ibid., pp. 101-114.

8. Knappert, Jan. *An Encyclopedia of Myth and Legend: Indian Mythology*. New Delhi, India: HarperCollins, 1992, p. 180.

9. Ibid., pp. 30, 96.

10. Klostermaier, Klaus K. The Beginnings of Hinduism. In *Hinduism, a Short History*. Oxford: Oneworld Publications, 2000, pp. 35-45.

11. Subramaniam, Kamala. *Srimad Bhagavatam*. Mumbai, India: Bharatiya Vidya Bhavan, 1987, pp. 86-91.

12. *An Encyclopedia of Myth and Legend*, p. 233.

13. Pandey, Rajbali. *Hindu Samskaras*. New Delhi, India: Motilal Banarsidass Publishers Pvt. Ltd., 1969, pp. 111-113.

14. Danielou, Alain. *Gods of Love and Ecstasy: The Traditions of Shiva and Dionysus*. Rochester, VT: Inner Traditions, 1992, p. 96.

Chapter 3

1. Information from a Web site on Tirumala-Tirupati, <http://www.tirupati.org>.

2. Ambalal, Amit. *Krishna As Srinathji*. Ahmadabad, India: Mapin Publishing Pvt. Ltd., 1995, p. 160.

3. Walker, Benajmin. God. In *Hindu World*, Volume 1. New Delhi, India: Munishiram Manoharlal Publishers Pvt. Ltd., 1983, pp. 393-397.

4. Flood, Gavin. *An Introduction to Hinduism*. New Delhi, India: Cambridge University Press, 1998, pp. 17-21.

5. *Ramakian [Ramayana]*. The Government Lottery Office of Thailand, 1995.

6. O'Flaherty, Wendy Doniger. *The Origins of Evil in Hindu Mythology*. New Delhi, India: Motilal Banarsidass Publishers Pvt. Ltd., 1988.

7. *Hindu World*, Volume 1, pp. 252-255.

8. Information from a Web site on the goddess Shri Mahalasa Narayani, <http://www.mahalasa.org>.

9. Doniger, Wendy. *Splitting the Difference*. New Delhi, India: Oxford University Press, 2000, p. 265.

10. Bhoothanadha Puranam quoted in the Web site <http://www.saranamayyappa.org/harikochat3.htm>.

11. Information from a Web site listing temples of Ayyappa, <www.ayyappan-ldc.com/index1.html>.

12. Information from a Web site on Ayyappa, <http://www.ayyappan.com/history/>.

13. Varma, Pavan K. *Krishna, the Playful Divine*. New Delhi, India: Penguin Books, 1993.

14. Hartsuiker, Dolf. *Sadhus, Holy Men of India*. London: Thames and Hudson, 1993, pp. 58-59.

15. Bhandarkar, Ramkrishna Gopal. *Vaisnavism, Saivism and Minor Religious Sytems*. New Delhi, India: Asian Educational Services, 1983, p. 122.

16. Devi, Shankuntala. *The World of Homosexuals*. New Delhi, India: Bell Books, 1978, pp. 145-147.

17. Kinsley, David. Radha. In *Hindu Goddesses, Visions of the Divine Feminine in the Hindu Religious Tradition*. New Delhi, India: Motilal Banarsidass Publishers Pvt. Ltd., 1987, pp. 81-94.

18. Ibid., pp. 81-94.

19. C.S. Lakshmi heads an organization called Sparrow, which compiles oral histories of Indian women.

20. Niklas, Ulrike. *The Mystery of the Threshold: "Ali" of Southern India*. A documentary project in collaboration with Pondicherry University (Indo-German Project of Cultural Anthropology) with the support of Deutscher Akademischer Austavschdienst (DAAD). A Preliminary Account reported in <http://www.rrz.uni-koeln.de/phil-fak/indologie/kolam/kolam1/alieng.html>.

21. Kinsley, David. Village Goddesses. In *Hindu Goddesses, Visions of the Divine Feminine in the Hindu Religious Tradition*. New Delhi, India: Motilal Banarsidass Publishers Pvt. Ltd., 1987, pp. 197-208.

22. Walker, Benajmin. Aeons. In *Hindu World*, Volume 1. New Delhi, India: Munishiram Manoharlal Publishers Pvt. Ltd., 1983, pp. 6-9.

23. Sen, Makhan Lal. *The Ramayana of Valmiki*. New Delhi, India: Munishiram Manoharlal Publishers Pvt. Ltd., 1978, p. 322.

Chapter 4

1. Doniger, Wendy. *Splitting the Difference*. New Delhi, India: Oxford University Press, 2000, p. 279.

2. Jaini, Padmanabh S. *Mahabharata* Motifs in the *Jaina Pandava Purana*. In *Collected Papers on Jaina Studies*. New Delhi, India: Motilal Banarsidass Publishers Pvt. Ltd., 2000, p. 355.

3. O'Flaherty, Wendy Doniger. *Sexual Metaphors and Animal Symbols in Indian Mythology*. New Delhi, India: Motilal Banarsidass Publishers Pvt. Ltd., 1981, p. 310.

4. Personal communication with Professor John Smith, University of Cambridge, who worked on the classical edition of the *Mahabharata*.

5. Randolph, P., Lundschen, Conner, Sparks, David Hatfield, Sparks, Mariya. Agdistis, Attis. In *Cassell's Encyclopedia of Queer Myth, Symbol, and Spirit*. London: Cassel, 1997, pp. 44, 76.

6. Kinsley, David. Village Goddesses. In *Hindu Goddesses, Visions of the Divine Feminine in the Hindu Religious Tradition*. New Delhi, India: Motilal Banarsidass Publishers Pvt. Ltd., 1987, pp. 197-208.

7. Ramanujan, A.K. The Indian Oedipus. In Dharwadker, Vinay, ed. *The Collected Essays of A.K. Ramanujan*. New Delhi, India: Oxford University Press, 1999, p. 387.

8. Meyer, Johann Jakob. *Sexual Life in Ancient India*. New Delhi, India: Motilal Banarsidass Publishers Pvt. Ltd., 1989, p. 480.

9. *Cassell's Encyclopedia of Queer Myth, Symbol, and Spirit,* p. 192.

10. Walker, Benajmin. Prostitution. In *Hindu World,* Volume 2. New Delhi, India: Munishiram Manoharlal Publishers Pvt. Ltd., 1983, p. 246.

11. Ramanujan, A.K. The Prince Who Married His Own Left Half. In Dharwadker, Vinay, ed. *The Collected Essays of A.K. Ramanujan*. New Delhi, India: Oxford University Press, 1999, pp. 409-410.

12. Subramaniam, Kamala. *Srimad Bhagavatam*. Mumbai, India: Bharatiya Vidya Bhavan, 1987, pp. 55-56.

Chapter 5

1. Nabar, V. and Tumkur, S., tr. Chapter 11. In *The Bhagavadgita*. Hertfordshire, England: Wordsworth, 1997, pp. 48-53.

2. Martin-Dubost, Paul. *Ganesha: Enchanter of the Three Worlds*. Mumbai, India: Franco-Indian Research, 1997, p. 62.

3. Cohen, Lawrence. The Wives of Ganesha. In Brown, Robert L. ed. *Ganesh—Studies of an Asian God*. Delhi, India: Sri Satguru, 1991, p. 118.

4. Meyer, Johann Jakob. *Sexual Life in Ancient India*. New Delhi, India: Motilal Banarsidass Publishers Pvt. Ltd., 1989, p. 369.

5. *Ganesh*—Studies of an Asian God, p. 136.

6. Ramanujan, A.K. The Indian Oedipus. In Dharwadker, Vinay, ed. *The Collected Essays of A.K. Ramanujan*. New Delhi, India: Oxford University Press, 1999, p. 384.

7. Frawley, David. *From the River of Heaven*. New Delhi, India: Motilal Banarsidass Publishers Pvt. Ltd., 1992, pp. 101-106.

8. *Sexual Life in Ancient India,* p. 368.

9. Jaini, Padmanabh S. *The Jaina Path of Purification*. New Delhi, India: Motilal Banarsidass Publishers Pvt. Ltd., 1979, p. 131.

10. Kulkarnia, V.M. *The Story of Rama in Jain Literature*. Ahmadabad, India: Saraswati Pustak Bhandar, 1990, p. 40.

11. Walker, Benajmin. Gender. In *Hindu World,* Volume 1. New Delhi, India: Munishiram Manoharlal Publishers Pvt. Ltd., 1983, pp. 388-389.

12. O'Flaherty, Wendy Doniger. *Sexual Metaphors and Animal Symbols in Indian Mythology*. New Delhi, India: Motilal Banarsidass Pub. Pvt. Ltd., 1981, pp. 323.

13. Danielou, Alain. *Gods of Love and Ecstasy: The Traditions of Shiva and Dionysus.* Rochester, VT: Inner Traditions, 1992, pp. 76-85.

14. Doniger, Wendy. *Splitting the Difference.* New Delhi, India: Oxford University Press, 2000, p. 247.

Glossary

acharya: Teacher.

Agni: Fire-god.

Ali: Organized communities of transvestites, transsexuals, and eunuchs in Tamil Nadu.

Amba: Princess of Kashi; Shikhandi in his former life.

Apsara: Nymph who seduces sages.

artha: Worldly wealth.

Arya: Noble man who respects dharma, practices yoga, performs yagna, and respects the *Vedas*.

ashrama: Stage of life: student, householder, retired teacher, and hermit.

Asuras: Enemies of the Devas; demons who live in the nether regions; sons of Kashyapa born of Diti.

ayonija: Born without being nurtured in the womb.

Ayurveda: Ancient Indian medical system.

Ayyappa: Celibate son of Shiva and Vishnu who is worshipped in Kerala.

B.C.E.: Before common era, formerly referred to as B.C.

Bhagavan: Godhead; he who rotates the cycle of life.

Bhisma: Title bestowed upon Devavrata; Granduncle of the Pandavas and Kauravas.

bhola: Without guile; a quality of Shiva.

Bodhisattva: An enlightened Buddhist being who can break free from the cycle of life but chooses to stay back to help other suffering beings.

Brahma: Creator; sits on a lotus, chants the Vedas from his four heads, and holds implements to perform yagna in his four hands; not worshipped because he desired his daughter, the primal female.

brahmachari: One who practices brahmacharya; student.

brahmacharya: Chaste student life; first stage of life.

brahman: Ultimate divine principle that is undefinable, changeless, eternal, and infinite according to the *Upanishads*.

Brahmana: Ritual texts based on Vedic hymns.

Brahma-vidya: Knowledge of the Absolute.

Brahmin: Highest ritual caste; priest and philosopher; those who teach society.

Brihaspati: Lord of the planet Jupiter.

Buddha: An enlightened being who has broken free from the cycle of life; specifically refers to Siddhartha Gautama, founder of the Buddhist monastic order.

Buddhism: The agnostic religion founded by the Buddha; believes desire is the cause of suffering and meditation generates restraint that helps one triumph over suffering and attain nirvana (freedom from the wheel of existence).

Budha: Lord of the planet Mercury; son of the moon-god.

C.E.: Common era, formerly referred to as A.D.

chakra: Gateways to occult knowledge; seven located along the spine; roused through Tantrik practices.

Chandra: The moon-god.

chthonian: Creatures bound to earth, to Nature, and subject to material transformations; opposite of celestial.

Dakini: Witch; mistress of occult lore.

Daksha: A mind-born son of Brahma; father-in-law of all the gods including Shiva; lord of Dakshinachara.

Dakshinachara: Conventional, mainstream, ritualistic way of life based on rituals and philosophies inspired by the *Vedas;* this approach views the material world as wild and illusory that needs to be restrained through dharma and yoga.

demiurge: Primal source.

desi: Folk; parochial.

Deva: Enemies of the Asuras; gods who live in the celestial regions; sons of Kashyapa, born of Aditi.

devadasis: Servants of god; temple prostitutes.

Devavrata: Granduncle of Pandavas and Kauravas who chose to remain celibate so that his father Shantanu could marry the woman he loved.

dharma: Social order based on the doctrine of duty instituted and maintained by Vishnu.

Draupadi: Common-wife of the five Pandavas.

Drona: Preceptor of the Kuru clan; teacher of the Kauravas and Pandavas; friend and later foe of Drupada.

Drupada: Father of Shikhandi, Draupadi, and Dhristadhyumna; friend and later foe of Drona.

Durga: Warrior manifestation of the mother-goddess; dressed in red, riding a lion, bearing weapons in her eight arms she kills the buffalo-demon.

dvija: Twice-born; term used to refer to an initiated member of the upper caste (specifically a Brahmin).

Gandharvas: Celestial musicians; companions of Apsaras.

Ganesha: Elephant-headed son of Gauri; remover of obstacles; adored as a bachelor in southern India, but has two wives in northern Indian traditions.

Gauri: Wife of Shiva; another name for Parvati; radiant and maternal manifestation of the mother-goddess.

gharana: Household; clan.

gopi: Milkmaid.

grihastha: Householder; second stage of life.

grihasthi: He who practices grahastha; householder.

Hanuman: Monkey-god who serves Rama.

Hara: Another name for Shiva.

Hari: Another name for Vishnu.

Hijras: Organized communities of transvestites, transsexuals, and eunuchs in northern India.

Hindu: Generic term for a set of beliefs, customs, and practices that evolved in the Indian subcontinent and later spread to Southeast Asia; has two approaches to life the Vedic and Tantrik; is divided into three theistic schools based on the worship of Shiva (Shaiva), Vishnu (Vaishnava), and the mother-goddess (Shakta).

Ikshavaku: Son of Manu; founder of the solar line of kings.

Ila: Son/daughter of Manu; founder of the lunar line of kings.

Indra: King of the Devas; god of the sky, rain, and thunder.

Itihasa: Legendary history; *Ramayana, Mahabharata,* and its appendix, "Harivamsa."

Jainism: The atheistic religion based on austerities and nonviolence that rejects Vedic ritualism and helps aspirant generate good karma enabling him/her to attain kaivalya (freedom from the cycle of life).

jati: Caste.

kaivalya: Jain concept of liberation from the cycle of life; isolation from impurities; omniscience that liberates one from the cycle of life.

Kali: Wild and fierce manifestation of the mother-goddess.

Kama: God of love and lust who wields a sugarcane bow, shoots flowery darts, and rides a parrot.

kama: Desire, love, lust.

Kannada: Indian language spoken in the southwestern state of Karnataka.

karma: Action one performs as well as reactions of those actions that one is bound to experience either in this life or the next.

Kartikeya: Son of Shiva; the warlord who killed an Asura on the seventh day of his life; rides a peacock, wields a lance, and has a rooster-insignia on his banner; is said to be a bachelor in northern India and has two wives—Valli and Sena—in southern India.

Kauravas: Villains in the *Mahabharata;* enemies of the Pandavas who believe they have a greater right to the throne of Hastinapur because their father Dhritarashtra, though blind and deemed unfit to rule, was the elder son of Vichitravirya.

Kimnara: Literally, what men; quasi-men; "queer" beings.

Kimpurusha: Literally, what men; quasi-men; "queer" beings.

kliba: Non-man, which means hermaphrodite, impotent man, homosexual man, sterile man, man who cannot do what a man is supposed to do, man who does not desire women; sexually dysfunctional male; eunuch.

kothi: Traditional gender construct in India for males who prefer to have sex with men and/or are effeminate and/or are passive sex partners.

Krishna: Human incarnation of Vishnu who established dharma in the third quarter of the world cycle; renowned for his beauty, charm, and his winsome wiliness; godhead personified.

Krittika: Nursemaids of Kartikeya.

Kshatriya: Second highest ritual caste; warrior and administrator; those who rule and protect society.

Kuru: The clan of warriors to which the Pandavas and Kauravas belong.

Laxmana: Rama's younger brother.

Laxmi: Goddess of wealth and fortune; wears red sari and gold ornaments and sits on a lotus with lotuses and a pot in her hand.

Liminal: Between two worlds or ideas.

linga: Phallus.

mage: Ancestor, originator.

Mahabharata: Epic based on the struggle between the Pandavas and Kauravas for the throne of Hastinapur.

Mahavidya: Wise, autonomous, feared goddess.

Manavas: Children of Manu; humans.

Mangal: Lord of the planet Mars; Kartikeya.

mantra: Sacred or mystical chant.

Manu: Father of humankind.

margi: Classical; Brahmanical.

Masti: Fun, mischief.

Matrika: Wild mothers of the forest.

matsya nyaya: Law of the fishes where big fish eat the small fish; refers to the law of the jungle where might is right.

maya: Delusion; misinterpretation of sensory stimuli by an unenlightened mind.

Mohini: Celestial enchantress.

moksha: Hindu concept of liberation from the cycle of life.

murath: Term common in northern India for kothi.

Murugan: Another name for Kartikeya that is popular in Tamil Nadu.

Nagas: Serpent beings who live in subterranean realms.

namard: Non-man (*see also* Kliba).

napunsaka: Non-man (*see also* Kliba).

Narada: Mind-born son of Brahma; devotee of Vishnu; renowned for his meddlesome nature.

naraka: Subterranean realm of Asuras.

Narasimha: Half-man, half-lion incarnation of Vishnu.

natha: Master, lord, teacher, guru.

nirvana: Buddhist concept of liberation from the cycle of life; blowing out of impermanent constructs.

ojas: Spiritual energy radiating from retained semen.

outcaste: Lowest rank in the Hindu caste hierarchy.

paap: Conduct that goes against dharma and generates unfavorable karma.

Pandavas: Heroes in the *Mahabharata;* enemies of the Kauravas who believe they have a greater right to the throne of Hastinapur because their father Pandu, though the younger son of Vichitravirya, was crowned king.

panthi: Traditional gender construct in India for males who do not mind having sex with kothis, are masculine, and are active sex partners.

parakiya: Belonging to another; tradition where Krishna's beloved Radha is the wife of another man.

parampara: Tradition.

Parvati: Consort of Shiva; princess of the mountains; succeeded in making the hermit Shiva a householder.

Pitrs: Forefathers.

Prajapati: Father of beings; another name for Brahma or his manifestation, Kashyapa.

prakriti: Nature; another term for material reality or samsara.

Prithu: The sovereign who domesticated the earth and established dharma; incarnation of Vishnu.

Punya: Conduct that upholds dharma and generates favorable karma.

Puranas: Ancient chronicles of gods, kings, and sages written between 500 and 1500 C.E.

Puru: Ancestor of the Kurus; accepted his father Yayati's old age so that Yayati could enjoys the pleasures of youth.

Purusha: Primal man; another term for spiritual reality.

purushartha: Validation of human life through ethical (dharma), economic (artha), sensual (kama), and spiritual (moksha) activities.

Put: Land of suffering reserved for childless men.

put-ra: Son; deliverer form the realm known as Put.

put-ri: Daughter; deliverer form the realm known as Put.

Radha: Beloved of Krishna; a milkmaid; believed to be the wife of another man in one tradition and the shakti of Krishna in another.

rajas: Agitative quality of matter.

Rakshasas: Demons; barbarians; wild forest spirits.

Ramayana: Epic based on the life of Rama.

Ravana: King of the Rakshasa; villain of the Ramayana; abducted Sita and was killed by Rama.

Rishi: Seer; wise men who transmitted cosmic knowledge to humankind through Vedic hymns.

Sakhi-bhava: Emotion of identifying oneself as a female companion of the lord (specifically as the handmaidens of Radha, the beloved of Krishna).

samadhi: Yogic term for breaking free from the cycle of life by discriminating between material and spiritual reality.

sampradaya: Religious order.

samsara: Material reality; wheel of existence; cycle of rebirths; Nature; mundane world of time and space, name and form.

sanyasa: Hermit; fourth and final stage of life.

sanyasi: He who practices sanyasa; hermit.

Saraswati: Goddess of learning and the arts; consort of Brahma; draped in white sari, holds a lute, a pen, a book, and rides a gander.

Sati: First wife of Shiva who killed herself when her father Daksha insulted her husband by not inviting him to the sacrifice.

sattva: Harmonius quality of matter.

Shaivas: Devotees of Shiva.

Shakti: Goddess who embodies material energy.

shakti: Divine power embodied in female form.

shastra: Scriptures that help humans live a full life (*see also* Puru-shartha).

shauk: Hobby, pleasurable pastime.

Shikhandi: Male form of Shikhandini.

Shikhandini: Drupada's daughter who was raised as a son; Amba in her next life.

Shiva: Cosmic-hermit; god of destruction; wears animal skins, smears his body with ash, meditates on icy mountains, dances in crematoriums, smokes hemp, carries a trident, and rides a bull; world renouncing aspect of godhead.

shraadh: Ceremony to offer funerary offerings to forefathers.

shruti: Divine revelations; the *Vedas.*

Shudra: Lowest ritual caste; servants and laborers; those who serve society.

Shukra: Lord of the planet Venus.

siddha: He who attains siddhi.

siddhi: Mystical powers that enable a man manipulate cosmic forces.

Sita: Chaste wife of Rama.

smriti: Scriptures based on human memory that inform man how to live wholesome lives; include the *Puranas* and the *shastras.*

Sthala Purana: Local chronicles.

Subramaniam: Another name for Kartikeya popular in southern India.

Sugriva: King of the monkeys or Vanars.

Surya: The sun-god.

svakiya: Belonging to the same; tradition where Radha is one half of Krishna.

swarga: Celestial realms; abode of the Devas.

swayamvara: Practice of letting women choose their own husband.

tamas: Inert quality of matter.

tantra: Occult side of Hinduism (*see also* Vamachara) that views the flesh and the material world as the medium through which the truth can be realized.

Tantrik: Occult side of Hinduism, where the material world is viewed as energy (shakti), where sensory stimulation is sought, and mainstream taboos are violated in the quest to gain spiritual power (*see also* Vamachara).

Tirthankara: Supreme Jain soul who has attained kaivalya and liberated himself from the material world after following the Jain doctrines.

Upa Purana: Minor chronicles of gods, kings, and sages.

upanayana: Thread ceremony; rite of passage that makes a Brahmin boy ready for Vedic instruction.

Upanishads: Philosophical treatises based on the *Vedas*, which seek the ultimate truth.

uttarayana: Journey of the rising sun along the horizon in the northern direction from winter solstice to the summer solstice; opposite of dakshinyana.

Vaishnava: Devotees of Vishnu.

Vaishya: Third highest ritual caste; farmers, herdsmen, craftsmen, and traders; those who provide for society.

Vali: Brother of Sugriva.

vama: Left.

Vamachara: Unconventional, occult Tantrik way of life.

vamangi: Wife; she who sits on the left side.

vanaprastha: Retired teacher; third stage of life.

Vanara: Monkey; literally means forest dweller.

varna: Four ritual castes: those who teach, protect, provide, and serve society.

Varuna: Vedic god of morality who later became renowned as the lord of the sea.

Vedas: Collection of hymns that capture the absolute truth.

Vedic: Ritualistic, speculative, and mainstream Hinduism, where Nature is viewed as something wild to be regulated by dharma and where the material world is seen as a delusion that overwhelms the senses. Truth can be realized only through mental control (yoga) (*see also* Dakshinachara).

Vena: A king who abandoned dharma.

vichitra: Odd; queer.

Vidyadhara: Keepers of occult lore.

Vinayaka: He who was born without the aid of a man; another name of Ganesha.

vira: Heroic being; brave conqueror of spiritual or material realms; refers to both the sage and the warrior.

virya: Semen; manliness; virility; male essence.

Vishnu: Cosmic-king; god who sustains the world by instituting and maintaining dharma; adorns himself with silk, garlands, jewels, and sandal paste; rests on a serpent and rides an eagle; world-affirming aspect of godhead.

yagna: Vedic ritual involving chanting of hymns to invoke Devas and offering of oblations into the fire altar so that the cosmos function in one's favor.

Yakshas: Forest spirits associated with money and magic.

yantra: Sacred diagram.

Yellamma: Everyone's mother; village-goddess whose head and body belong to different castes; goddess associated with ritual prostitution.

Yoga: Mystical side of Hinduism; prevents the mind from being overwhelmed by the charms of the material world.

yogi: He who practices yoga; mystic.

Yogini: Priestess of occult lore.

yoni: Womb; female generative organ.

Bibliography

Abbot, J.E. and Godbole, N.R. *Stories of Indian Saints*. New Delhi, India: Motilal Banarsidass Publishers Pvt. Ltd., 1996.

Ambalal, Amit. *Krishna As Srinathji*. Ahmadabad, India: Mapin Publishing Pvt. Ltd., 1995.

Anderson, Leona M. *Vasantotsava: The Spring Festivals of India*. New Delhi, India: D.K. Printworld (P) Ltd., 1993.

Bagemihl, Bruce. *Biological Exuberance and Animal Homosexuality and Natural Diversity*. London: Profile Books, 1999.

Bhandarkar, Ramkrishna Gopal. *Vaisnavism, Saivism and Minor Religious Systems*. New Delhi, India: Asian Educational Services, 1983.

Bhattacharji, Sukumari. *The Indian Theogony*. New Delhi, India: Penguin Books, 2000.

Bristow, Joseph. *Sexuality* [the new critical idiom series]. London: Routledge, 1997.

Brown, Robert L. ed. *Ganesh—Studies of an Asian God*. New Delhi, India: Sri Satguru, 1991.

Coupe, Lawrence. *Myth* [the new critical idiom series]. London: Routledge, 1997.

Courtright, Paul B. *Ganesha: Lord of Obstacles, Lord of Beginnings*. New York: Oxford University Press, 1985.

Dange, Sadashiv Ambadas. *Encyclopaedia of Puranic Beliefs and Practices,* Volumes I-V. New Delhi, India: Navran, 1990.

Danielou, Alain. *Gods of Love and Ecstasy: The Traditions of Shiva and Dionysus*. Rochester, VT: Inner Traditions, 1992.

Devi, Shakuntala. *The World of Homosexuals*. New Delhi, India: Bell Books, 1978.

Dhal, Upendra Nath. *Goddess Lakshmi: Origin and Development*. New Delhi, India: Eastern Book Linkers, 1995.

Dharwadker, Vinay, ed. *The Collected Essays of A.K. Ramanujan*. New Delhi, India: Oxford University Press, 1999.

Doniger, Wendy. *Splitting the Difference*. New Delhi, India: Oxford University Press, 2000.

Doniger, Wendy and Smith, Brain K. *The Laws of Manu*. New Delhi, India: Penguin Books, 1991.

Eliot, Alexander. *The Universal Myths*. New York: Meridian Books, 1990.

Entwistle, A.W. *Braj, Centre of Krishna Pilgrimage*. Groningen, Netherlands: Egbert Forsten, 1987.

Flood, Gavin. *An Introduction to Hinduism*. New Delhi, India: Cambridge University Press, 1998.

Frawley, David. *From the River of Heaven*. New Delhi, India: Motilal Banarsidass Publishers Pvt. Ltd., 1992.

Graves, Robert. *The Greek Myths*. London: Penguin Books, 1960.

Haberman, David L. *Journey Through the Twelve Forests: An Encounter with Krishna*. New York: Oxford University Press, 1994.

Hartsuiker, Dolf. *Sadhus, Holy Men of India*. London: Thames and Hudson, 1993.

Highwater, Jamake. *Myth & Sexuality*. New York: Meridian, 1990.

Hiltebeitel, Alf. *The Cult of Draupadi*. Chicago: The University of Chicago Press, 1988.

Holmstrom, Lakshmi. *Silappadikaram, Manimekalai*. Hyderabad, India: Orient Longman, 1996.

Hopcke, R.H., Carrington, K.L., and Wirth, S., eds. *Same-Sex Love*. Boston: Shambala, 1993.

Jagannathan, Shakunthala and Krishna, Nanditha. *Ganesha: The Auspicious. . . the Beginning*. Mumbai, India: Vakil, Feffer and Simons, 1992.

Jaini, Padmanabh S. *The Jaina Path of Purification*. New Delhi, India: Motilal Banarsidass Publishers Pvt. Ltd., 1979.

Jakimowicz-Shah, Marta. *Metamorphosis of Indian Gods*. Calcutta: Seagull Books, 1988.

Jayakar, Pupul. *The Earth Mother*. New Delhi: Penguin Books, 1989.

Jordan, Michael. *Myths of the World*. London: Cambridge University Press, 1993.

Karve, Iravati. *Yuganta: The End of an Epoch*. Hyderabad, India: Disha Books, 1991.

Kinsley, David. *Hindu Goddesses, Visions of the Divine Feminine in the Hindu Religious Tradition*. New Delhi, India: Motilal Banarsidass Publishers Pvt. Ltd., 1987.

Klostermaier, Klaus K. *Hinduism, a Short History*. Oxford: Oneworld Publications, 2000.

Knappert, Jan. *An Encyclopedia of Myth and Legend: Indian Mythology*. New Delhi, India: HarperCollins, 1992.

Kramrisch, Stella. *The Presence of Shiva*. New Delhi, India: Motilal Banarsidass Publishers Pvt. Ltd., 1988.

Mani, Vettam. *Puranic Encyclopaedia*. New Delhi, India: Motilal Banarsidass Publishers Pvt. Ltd., 1996.

Martin-Dubost, Paul. *Ganesha: Enchanter of the Three Worlds*. Mumbai, India: Franco-Indian Research, 1997.

Mazumdar, Subash. *Who's Who in the* Mahabharata. Mumbai, India: Bharatiya Vidya Bhavan, 1988.

Merchant, Hoshan, ed. *Yaraana: Gay Writing in India.* New Delhi, India: Penguin Books, 1999.

Meyer, Johann Jakob. *Sexual Life in Ancient India.* New Delhi, India: Motilal Banarsidass Publishers Pvt. Ltd., 1989.

Nabar, V., Tumkur, S., tr. *The Bhagavad Gita.* Hertfordshire, England: Wordsworth Classics, 1997.

Nanda, Serena. *Neither Man nor Woman: The Hijras of India.* Belmont, CA: Wadsworth, 1990.

O'Flaherty, Wendy Doniger, tr. *Hindu Myths.* New Delhi, India: Penguin Books, 1975.

O'Flaherty, Wendy Doniger, tr. *Rig Veda: An Anthology.* New Delhi, India: Penguin Books, 1994.

O'Flaherty, Wendy Doniger. *Sexual Metaphors and Animal Symbols in Indian Mythology.* New Delhi, India: Motilal Banarsidass Publishers Pvt. Ltd., 1981.

O'Flaherty, Wendy Doniger. *Shiva: The Erotic Ascetic.* London: Oxford University Press Paperbacks, 1981.

Panati, Charles. *Sexy Origins and Intimate Things.* New York: Penguin Books, 1998.

Pandey, Rajbali. *Hindu Samskaras.* New Delhi, India: Motilal Banarsidass Publishers Pvt. Ltd., 1969.

Randolph, P., Lundschen, Conner, Hatfield Sparks, David and Sparks, Mariya. *Cassell's Encyclopedia of Queer Myth, Symbol, and Spirit.* London: Cassel, 1997.

Schwartz, Kit. *The Male Member.* New York: St. Martin's Press, 1985.

Sen, Makhan Lal. *The Ramayana of Valmiki.* New Delhi, India: Munishiram Manoharlal Publishers Pvt. Ltd., 1978.

Spencer, Colin. *Homosexuality: A History.* London: Fourth Estate, 1995.

Subramaniam, Kamala. *Mahabharata.* Mumbai, India: Bharatiya Vidya Bhavan, 1988.

Subramaniam, Kamala. *Ramayana.* Mumbai, India: Bharatiya Vidya Bhavan, 1990.

Subramaniam, Kamala. *Srimad Bhagavatam.* Mumbai, India: Bharatiya Vidya Bhavan, 1987.

Thadani, Giti. *Sakhiyani.* London: Cassell, 1996.

Vanita, Ruth and Kidwai, Saleem, eds. *Same-Sex Love in India: Readings from Literature and History.* New York: St. Martin's Press, 2000.

Varma, Pavan K. *Krishna, the Playful Divine.* New Delhi, India: Penguin Books, 1993.

Walker, Benajmin. *Hindu World,* Volumes 1 and 2. New Delhi, India: Munishiram Manoharlal Publishers Pvt. Ltd., 1983.

Wilkins, W.J. *Hindu Mythology.* New Delhi, India: Rupa & Co, 1997.

Zaehner, R.C. *Hindu Scriptures.* New Delhi, India: Rupa & Co, 1995.

Zimmer, Heinrich. *Myths and Symbols in Indian Art and Civilization.* New Delhi, India: Motilal Banarsidass Publishers Pvt. Ltd., 1990.

Index

Abhimanyu, 96
Achilles, 2
Adi, 73-74
Adishakti, 127-128
Adityas. *See* Devas
adultery
    accusations of, 62
    avoided, 91, 92, 97, 106
    examples of, 50, 51, 63, 81, 91
    psychoanalysis of, 131
    punishment for, 104, 105, 107
Agastya, 54
Agni, 61-62, 74
Agni Purana, 74
Ahalya, 49-50, 105-106
Ailas, 46, 47
Amar Chitra Katha comic books
    Ayyappa, 75
    demons in, 68
    Elephanta, 71
    Ganesha, 115, 116
    Ghatotkacha, 84
Amba. *See also* Shikhandi
    Bhisma and, 23-24
    rebirth of, 24, 26, 60
    sex change of, 32-33, 37, 40
    Shikhandi and, 19-20, 35
    Shiva invoked by, 24, 27-28
Ambalal, Amit, 82
Ambalika, 23, 25
Ambika, 23, 25
Anand, Subhash, 57
androgyny
    adoration of, 5
    of Ardhanareshwara, 122-123,
        124-130
    as aspect of maleness, 14, 129
    of Ganesha, 116-120
    hermaphrodites, 11, 120
    in India, 10-16
    serial, 45-47

Annamalai, Shri, 109
Apsaras. *See* nymphs
Araka, 83
Aravan, 87-88
Ardhanareshwara, 3, 122-123, 124-130
Arjuna
    castration of, 13, 95-99
    in the Maharaas, 80-81
    in Pandava battle, 33-34, 83-84,
        97-98, 114-115
art
    fantastic beings in, 114
    masculinity in, 14, 59-60
    symbolism in, 59-60, 66, 124-125,
        129
    Tantrik, 118
Aruna, 49, 50
Aryans, 48-49, 55
Asanga, 44
asceticism, 59-64, 72, 76, 104, 111. *See
    also* celibacy; semen,
    retention of
Asuras, 57-58, 61-62, 67-70, 71
Atharva Veda, 56, 97
Avikshita, 22-23
ayonijas, 53-55, 60-62, 76, 115
Ayyappa, 16, 74-77

Bahuchara, 99-102
Beeja, 28-30
Beruni, Al, 6
Bhagavad Gita, 7, 21, 37, 67, 98
Bhagavata Purana
    Krishna in, 83
    Narasimha in, 113
    procreation in, 44-45, 55, 110
    rebirth in, 92
    serial androgyny in, 47
Bhandarkar, R. G., 79-80
Bhangashvana, King, 41-42

Order Your Own Copy of
This Important Book for Your Personal Library!

THE MAN WHO WAS A WOMAN AND OTHER QUEER TALES FROM HINDU LORE

_____in hardbound at $34.95 (ISBN: 1-56023-180-7)

_____in softbound at $17.95 (ISBN: 1-56023-181-5)

COST OF BOOKS_____

OUTSIDE USA/CANADA/
MEXICO: ADD 20%____

POSTAGE & HANDLING_____
*(US: $4.00 for first book & $1.50
for each additional book)*
*Outside US: $5.00 for first book
& $2.00 for each additional book)*

SUBTOTAL_____

in Canada: add 7% GST____

STATE TAX____
*(NY, OH & MIN residents, please
add appropriate local sales tax)*

FINAL TOTAL____
*(If paying in Canadian funds,
convert using the current
exchange rate, UNESCO
coupons welcome.)*

❑ **BILL ME LATER:** ($5 service charge will be added)
(Bill-me option is good on US/Canada/Mexico orders only;
not good to jobbers, wholesalers, or subscription agencies.)

❑ Check here if billing address is different from
shipping address and attach purchase order and
billing address information.

Signature_____

❑ **PAYMENT ENCLOSED: $**_____

❑ **PLEASE CHARGE TO MY CREDIT CARD.**

❑ Visa ❑ MasterCard ❑ AmEx ❑ Discover
❑ Diner's Club ❑ Eurocard ❑ JCB

Account # _____

Exp. Date_____

Signature_____

Prices in US dollars and subject to change without notice.

NAME_____

INSTITUTION_____

ADDRESS_____

CITY_____

STATE/ZIP_____

COUNTRY_____ COUNTY (NY residents only)_____

TEL_____ FAX_____

E-MAIL_____

May we use your e-mail address for confirmations and other types of information? ❑ Yes ❑ No
We appreciate receiving your e-mail address and fax number. Haworth would like to e-mail or fax special
discount offers to you, as a preferred customer. **We will never share, rent, or exchange your e-mail address
or fax number.** We regard such actions as an invasion of your privacy.

Order From Your Local Bookstore or Directly From
The Haworth Press, Inc.
10 Alice Street, Binghamton, New York 13904-1580 • USA
TELEPHONE: 1-800-HAWORTH (1-800-429-6784) / Outside US/Canada: (607) 722-5857
FAX: 1-800-895-0582 / Outside US/Canada: (607) 722-6362
E-mail: getinfo@haworthpressinc.com
PLEASE PHOTOCOPY THIS FORM FOR YOUR PERSONAL USE.
www.HaworthPress.com

BOF00